365 BUDDHA

365 BUDDHA

Daily Meditations

JEFF SCHMIDT

Jeremy P. Tarcher/Putnam

a member of Penguin Putnam Inc.

New York

Most Tarcher/Putnam books are available at special quantity discounts for bulk purchase for sales promotions, premiums, fund-raising, and educational needs. Special books or book excerpts also can be created to fit specific needs. For details, write Putnam Special Markets, 375 Hudson Street, New York, NY 10014.

Jeremy P. Tarcher/Putnam
a member of
Penguin Putnam Inc.
375 Hudson Street
New York, NY 10014
www.penguinputnam.com

Library of Congress Cataloging-in-Publication Data

365 Buddha : daily meditations / Jeff Schmidt.
p.   cm.
ISBN 1-58542-143-X
1. Buddhist devotional calendars.   2. Buddhist meditations.
I. Title: Three hundred and sixty five Buddha.
BQ5579 .T47   2002   2001045109
294.3'4432—dc21

Printed in the United States of America
1   3   5   7   9   10   8   6   4   2

Book design by Jennifer Ann Daddio

May all beings be happy.
May they be healthy.
May they be free from suffering!

PREFACE

Nothing new will be said here, nor have I any skill in composition. Therefore I do not imagine that I can benefit others. I have done this to perfume my own mind.

ŚĀNTIDEVA;
Bodhicaryāvatāra 1.2

My life is harder than other people's; at least it seems that way to me. I know it is easier than most people's lives, but it often doesn't feel like it. Even when I get the things I want or situations turn out the way I had planned, these victories are fleeting, since nothing is constant. Life is rarely convenient and never certain. Birth is unpleasant. Old age is unpleasant. Sickness and death are unpleasant. Being with things we dislike and being without the things we do like are both unpleasant. Suffering is the unfailing nature of all unenlightened experience. We expect the world to satisfy our desires, clinging to the idea that "someday everything will be as it should be."

Wanting things to be different from what they are is suffering. Attraction and aversion, greed and hatred, lust and ill will: These are the attachments that cause suffering. "I like that; I want more"—"I dislike this; make it stop": Letting go of these attachments is the end of suffering. Release from this unsatisfactory predicament is the goal of life, whether we are aware of it or not.

The Buddha found that the root cause of our dissatisfaction is ignorance. It is the ignorance of having the mistaken view that we exist in a dualistic world—a world in which we treat the abstract illusion of an individual self, and its dependent and equally abstract illusion of an external world, as though they are concrete realities. We believe that we can repair this illusory world, even with all its failings and constant change, and that then we will be happy. Buddhist practice shows us that this is not so. The only way to eliminate our suffering is to eliminate the underlying ignorance that is its cause.

The true nature of our experience is empty of enduring reality, and it is through the unmediated vision of this emptiness that we correct our mistaken views. Our experience is void rather than solid, and ultimately it is beyond the control of our self-made ego. Once the conceited notion of self-and-other is eliminated, the clear bliss of the real nature of conditioned existence can pierce through, revealing the deathless state, known as nirvāṇa. It is this quest that is at the heart of all Buddhist endeavor.

The path described by the Buddha is difficult and, by nature, clouded in confusion. This compilation is intended to help keep many of the truths, tricks, and traps, presented in the Buddhist tradition, in our minds throughout our waking day. This is a day book with one quotation to be read and ruminated on throughout the day for each day of the year. Of course, you may read it all the way through or thumb through it at random; indeed, the quotations are arranged in a random order. Each passage stands on its own and needs no further commentary, though some passages may require more thought than others to be understood. They are worthwhile statements of Buddhist doctrine, and I have included them because I consider them useful for practice and as good sources leading to further reading.

Buddhism is a diverse field of study, and I could not hope to present a balanced representation of the vast wealth of Buddhist writings. I have tried to provide selections that will offer the reader an opportunity to explore some new areas of interest. There are passages on morality, on meditation, and on the subtle and sometimes contradictory philosophies of different Buddhist traditions. I have chosen quotations from different schools of Buddhism, from different times and places, and have selected passages that are of different levels of accessibility. I have included a glossary at the end of the book for words and names not found in standard dictionaries.

In editing these quotations, I have taken the liberty of Americanizing the spellings of words that have British spellings in the original texts. For words that are not in English, I have left the spellings in the languages of the original quotations (e.g., nibbāna in Pali, nirvāṇa in Sanskrit, etc.), but have standardized the transliterations of the letters in each language (e.g., nirvāṇa rather than nirvana or nirvāna); I have not changed the transliterations in titles. The way in which words are used is the artistic expression of each author and translator; I have left the letter case as in the original, and I have retained the gender of translations, though it is not necessarily the gender of the original text or the gender-neutral standard that we have come to expect in current writing. Parentheses ( ) are from the original passages, words in brackets [ ] are my additions.

I would like to thank Joel Fotinos for his encouragement to compile this collection. I would also like to thank Brad Bohland for the use of his notes on some of the works cited. My patient and supportive wife, Allison Sylvest, has made many useful suggestions and has been a tireless sounding board throughout this process; I am glad to have this opportunity to thank her publicly.

I .

This mind is an uncertain thing. This body is uncertain. Together they are impermanent. Together they are a source of suffering. Together they are devoid of self. These, the Buddha pointed out, are neither a being, nor a person, nor a self, nor a soul, nor us, nor they. They are merely elements: earth, water, fire and wind. Elements only!

When the mind sees this, it will rid itself of attachment which holds that 'I' am beautiful, 'I' am good, 'I' am evil, 'I' am suffering, 'I' have, 'I' this or 'I' that. You will experience a state of unity, for you'll have seen that all of mankind is basically the same. There is no 'I'. There are only elements.

AJAHN CHAH; *BODHINYĀNA*

2.

A fool is happy
Until his mischief turns against him.
And a good man may suffer
Until his goodness flowers.

DHAMMAPADA 119–120

3.

In the same way that someone in the midst of a rough crowd guards a wound with great care, so in the midst of bad company should one always guard the wound that is the mind.

ŚĀNTIDEVA; *BODHICARYĀVATĀRA 5.19*

4.

The best scenery is nought-to-see—
That is the Mind-Essence of Illumination.

HUNDRED THOUSAND SONGS OF MILAREPA

5.

You cannot find Buddha nature by vivisection. Reality cannot be caught by thinking or feeling mind. Moment after moment to watch your breathing, to watch your posture, is true nature. There is no secret beyond this point.

SHUNRYU SUZUKI; *ZEN MIND, BEGINNER'S MIND*

6.

[I]ndulge in lust a little, and like the child it grows apace.

The wise man hates it therefore; who would take poison for food?
Every sorrow is increased and cherished by the offices of lust.

If there is no lustful desire, the risings of sorrow are not produced,
the wise man seeing the bitterness of sorrow, stamps out and de-
stroys the risings of desire. . . .

FO-SHO-HING-TSAN-KING 852–854

7.

All . . . phenomena are intrinsically void and yet this Mind with which they are identical is no mere nothingness.

HUANG PO; *ZEN TEACHING OF HUANG PO*

8.

The king said: 'When deeds are committed, Nāgasena, by one name-and-form, what becomes of those deeds?'

'The deeds would follow it, O king, like a shadow that never leaves it.'

'Can any one point out those deeds, saying: "Here are those deeds, or there"?'

'No.'

'Give me an illustration.'

'Now what do you think, O king? Can any one point out the fruits which a tree has not yet produced, saying: "Here they are, or there"?'

'Certainly not, Sir.'

'Just so, great king, so long as the continuity of life is not cut off, it is impossible to point out the deeds that are done.'

'Very good, Nāgasena!'

MILINDAPAÑHA 72

9.

Who would have thought that all things are the manifestation of the Essence of Mind!

THE SUTRA OF HUI NENG

10.

A man who has learned but little, grows old like an ox;
His flesh increases, but his wisdom, not.

DHAMMAPADA 152

11.

If this doctrine is not understood thoroughly,
The conception of an I prevails,
Hence come virtuous and non-virtuous actions
Which give rise to good and bad rebirths.

Therefore, as long as the doctrine removing
The conception of I is not known,
Take heed of the practices
Of giving, ethics, and patience.

NĀGĀRJUNA; *PRECIOUS GARLAND 124–125*

12.

Let there be nothing behind you; leave the future to one side. Do not clutch at what is left in the middle; then you will become a wanderer and calm.

SUTTA NIPĀTA 949

13.

Whoever lives looking for pleasure, exercising no restraint over
his senses,
Immoderate in his enjoyments, indolent, inert,
Him Māra overpowers, even as the wind overpowers a tree of little strength.

Whoever lives looking not for pleasure, exercising restraint over
his senses,
Moderate in his enjoyments, endowed with faith, exerting the
power of his will,
Him Māra does not overpower, even as the wind does not overpower a mountain of rock.

DHAMMAPADA 7–8

14.

When an ordinary enemy is banished from one country he may regain his strength abroad and then return to seek revenge. The inner enemy of delusion, however, is not able to do this. When delusion is completely abandoned it can never return again.

ŚĀNTIDEVA; *BODHICARYĀVATĀRA 4.45*

15.

What is "not thus"? It is your self. What is "thus"? It is the Buddhas.

DŌGEN; *RATIONAL ZEN*

16.

There is no meditative concentration for one who lacks wisdom, and no wisdom for one who lacks meditative concentration. One in whom are found both meditative concentration and wisdom is indeed close to Nibbāna.

DHAMMAPADA 372

17.

I alone will practice all that is wholesome. Those who are power-
less and under the control of karma and delusion are unable to
benefit themselves or attain their own purposes. Worldly people
are completely unable to make their lives meaningful. Therefore, I
shall practice what is wholesome for the benefit of all sentient
beings. While others are engaged in inferior and menial tasks in
which they encounter many difficulties, how can I sit here at peace
and do nothing? I must and shall benefit them, but without ever
succumbing to the poison of self-importance.

ŚĀNTIDEVA; *BODHICARYĀVATĀRA 7.49–7.51*

18.

Abandoning gossip, he abstains from gossip; he speaks at the right time, speaks what is fact, speaks on what is good, speaks on the Dhamma and the Discipline; at the right time he speaks such words as are worth recording, reasonable, moderate, and beneficial.

MAJJHIMA-NIKĀYA i.180

19.

If nothing is permanent,
What will be impermanent,
Permanent and impermanent,
Or neither?

NĀGĀRJUNA; *MŪLAMADHYAMAKA-KĀRIKĀ XXVII, 20*

20.

Pride and indifference shroud this heart, too, as the sun is obscured by the piled-up clouds; supercilious thoughts root out all modesty of mind, and sorrow saps the strongest will.

FO-SHO-HING-TSAN-KING 1809

21.

Devoid of form and color,
Excelling the sense realms,
Is this wondrous mind
Out-reaching words and phrases.

HUNDRED THOUSAND SONGS OF MILAREPA

22.

This dharma is such that it cannot be attained by groping or searching about. In the realm of seeing, knowledge perishes. At the moment of attaining, mind is surpassed.

DŌGEN; *MOON IN A DEWDROP*

23.

And those who have no mental vigilance,
Though they may hear the teachings, ponder them or meditate,
With minds like water seeping from a leaking jug,
Their learning will not settle in their memories.

ŚĀNTIDEVA; *BODHICARYĀVATĀRA 5.25*

24.

Monks, I say there is no wicked deed that may not be committed by . . . the human being who has transgressed in one thing. What one thing? I mean the intentional uttering of a falsehood.

ITIVUTTAKA 25

25.

If I had supernatural power, I could take you up to the Pure Land of Amitābha Buddha for a visit, or to the Kingdom of God if you are a Christian. I am sure that everything would be nice and clean there, with beautiful scenery. But once you were there, how would your footsteps be? Can you be sure that your footprints in the Pure Land would not show traces of worries and sorrows you carried from this saṃsāric, worldly life?

If you take your worries and sorrows along with you and set them on the Pure Land, you would defile the Pure Land and make it much less pure! To deserve the Pure Land, you must be able to take peaceful and anxiety-free steps right here on this saṃsāric ground.

THICH NHAT HANH; *GUIDE TO WALKING MEDITATION*

26.

[E]arnestly practice every good work.

FO-SHO-HING-TSAN-KING 1981

27.

Mind precedes all mental states. Mind is their chief; they are all mind-wrought. If with an impure mind a person speaks or acts, suffering follows him like the wheel that follows the foot of the ox.

Mind precedes all mental states. Mind is their chief; they are all mind-wrought. If with a pure mind a person speaks or acts, happiness follows him like his never-departing shadow.

DHAMMAPADA 1–2

28.

Actually, emptiness of mind is not even a state of mind, but the original essence of mind which Buddha and the Sixth Patriarch experienced. "Essence of mind," "original mind," "original face," "Buddha nature," "emptiness"—all these words mean the absolute calmness of our mind.

SHUNRYU SUZUKI; *ZEN MIND, BEGINNER'S MIND*

29.

Just as vessels made of clay by a potter all have breaking as their end, so is the life of mortals.

SUTTA NIPĀTA 577

30.

Look into the sphere of birthless mind!
Let dawn the enjoyment of ceaseless play!
When free of hope and fear—that's the result.
Why speak of birth and death?
Come to the natural, unmodified state!

DRINKING THE MOUNTAIN STREAM: SONGS OF

TIBET'S BELOVED SAINT, MILAREPA

31.

Our very nature is Buddha, and apart from this nature there is no other Buddha.

THE SUTRA OF HUI NENG

32.

If you remove (from conduct) the purpose of the mind, the bodily act is but as rotten wood; wherefore, regulate the mind, and then the body will spontaneously go right.

FO-SHO-HING-TSAN-KING 527

33.

Of slight account, monks, is the loss of such things as wealth. Miserable indeed among losses is the loss of wisdom.

Of slight account, monks, is the increase of such things as wealth. Chief of all the increases is that of wisdom.

ANGUTTARA-NIKĀYA i.15

34.

Right speech, harmlessness,
Restraint in speaking ill of others,
Moderation in food, at peace in remoteness and solitude,
Devotion to higher meditation.
This is the teaching of the Buddhas.

DHAMMAPADA 185

35.

[W]here there is no more being born or growing old, no more dying, no more falling from one existence and rising up in another, I declare that that end of the world is not by going to be known, seen, or reached. . . . But, . . . I declare not that there is any making an end of Ill without reaching world's end. Nay, . . . in this very fathom-long body, along with its perceptions and thoughts, I proclaim the world to be, likewise the origin of the world and the making of the world to end, likewise the practice going to the ending of the world.

ANGUTTARA-NIKĀYA ii.48

36.

If you turn your light inwardly, you will find what is esoteric within you.

THE SUTRA OF HUI NENG

37.

Now what, bhikkhus, is the All. It is just the eye and visible objects, the ear and sounds, the nose and odors, the tongue and tastes, the body and tangible objects, the mind and objects of the mind. This, bhikkhus, is called the All.

Now whoever should speak thus: "Setting aside this All I will proclaim another All," it would be mere talk on his part and on being questioned he would be unable to proceed and in addition, vexation [would] befall him. For what reason? It would not be within his scope, bhikkhus.

SAMYUTTA NIKĀYA XXXV. 23

38.

If we have . . . presence of mind then whatever work we do will be the very tool which enables us to know right and wrong continually. There's plenty of time to meditate, we just don't fully understand the practice, that's all. While sleeping we breathe, eating we breathe, don't we? Why don't we have time to meditate? Wherever we are we breathe. If we think like this then our life has as much value as our breath, wherever we are we have time.

AJAHN CHAH; *TASTE OF FREEDOM*

39.

What is this true meditation? It is to make everything: coughing, swallowing, waving the arms, motion, stillness, words, action, the evil and the good, prosperity and shame, gain and loss, right and wrong, into one single koan.

HAKUIN; *ZEN MASTER HAKUIN*

40.

In the face of reality's illumination
There is neither self nor other,
No duality, no division—void of identity
And yet neither void
Nor not void,
There's no perceiver at all.
Eh Ma! Until a mountain yogi
Has realized well the meaning of this,
He should not disparage cause and result!

DRINKING THE MOUNTAIN STREAM: SONGS OF
TIBET'S BELOVED SAINT, MILAREPA

41.

All those who suffer in the world do so because of their desire for their own happiness. All those happy in the world are so because of their desire for the happiness of others.

ŚĀNTIDEVA; *BODHICARYĀVATĀRA 8.129*

42.

For if this "I" is lasting and imperishable, then reason would teach it never can be changed. But now we see the marks of joy and sorrow, what room for constancy then is here?

FO-SHO-HING-TSAN-KING 1370

43.

The king said: 'Nāgasena, he who escapes reindividualization [rebirth], is it by reasoning that he escapes it?'

'Both by reasoning, your Majesty, and by wisdom, and by other good qualities.'

'But are not reasoning and wisdom surely much the same?'

'Certainly not. Reasoning is one thing, wisdom another. Sheep and goats, oxen and buffaloes, camels and asses have reasoning, but wisdom they have not.'

'Well put, Nāgasena!'

MILINDAPAÑHA 32

44.

Brief time have sons of men on earth to live.
Let the good man herein much trouble take.
Acting as were his turban all a-blaze.
There is no man to whom death cometh not.

SAMYUTTA NIKĀYA IV. 1, 9

45.

If the perfection of generosity
Were the alleviation of the world's poverty,
Then since beings are still starving now
In what manner did the previous Buddhas perfect it?

The perfection of generosity is said to be
The thought to give all beings everything,
Together with the fruit of such a thought.
Hence it is simply a state of mind.

ŚĀNTIDEVA; *BODHICARYĀVATĀRA 5.9–5.10*

46.

Like a beautiful brightly colored flower without fragrance
Is the well-spoken word without action.

Like a beautiful brightly colored flower full of fragrance
Is the well-spoken word and the deed that matches the word.

DHAMMAPADA 51–52

47.

What people expect to happen is always different from what actually happens. From this comes great disappointment; this is the way the world works.

SUTTA NIPĀTA 588

48.

The assertion that the effect and cause are similar
Is not acceptable.
The assertion that they are not similar
Is also not acceptable.

NĀGĀRJUNA; *MŪLAMADHYAMAKA-KĀRIKĀ IV, 6*

49.

The king said: 'What is the characteristic mark of reasoning, and what of wisdom?'

'Reasoning has always comprehension as its mark; but wisdom has cutting off.'

'But how is comprehension the characteristic of reasoning, and cutting off of wisdom? Give me an illustration.'

'You remember the barley reapers?'

'Yes, certainly.'

'How do they reap the barley?'

'With the left hand they grasp the barley into a bunch, and taking the sickle into the right hand, they cut it off with that.'

'Just even so, O king, does the recluse by his thinking grasp his mind, and by his wisdom cut off his failings. In this way is it that comprehension is the characteristic of reasoning, but cutting off of wisdom.'

'Well put, Nāgasena!'

MILINDAPAÑHA 32–33

50.

There are two kinds of suffering: the suffering that leads to more suffering and the suffering that leads to the end of suffering. If you are not willing to face the second kind of suffering, you will surely continue to experience the first.

AJAHN CHAH; *STILL FOREST POOL*

51.

If we are peaceful, if we are happy, we can smile and blossom like a flower, and everyone in our family, our entire society, will benefit from our peace.

THICH NHAT HANH; *BEING PEACE*

52.

The hostile multitudes are vast as space—
What chance is there that all should be subdued?
Let but this angry mind be overthrown
And every foe is then and there destroyed.

To cover all the earth with sheets of hide—
Where could such amounts of skin be found?
But simply wrap some leather round your feet,
And it's as if the whole earth had been covered!

Likewise, we can never take
And turn aside the outer course of things.
But only seize and discipline the mind itself,
And what is there remaining to be curbed?

ŚĀNTIDEVA; *BODHICARYĀVATĀRA 5.12–5.14*

53.

Be quick to do good.
If you are slow,
The mind, delighting in mischief,
Will catch you.

DHAMMAPADA 116

54.

By amending our mistakes, we get wisdom.
By defending our faults, we betray an unsound mind.

THE SUTRA OF HUI NENG

55.

If you are afraid of pain,
if you don't like it,
do nothing evil,
either openly or in secret.
For if you do,
even if you get up and run away
you won't escape its pain.
If you are afraid of pain,
if you don't like it,
take refuge in the Buddha,
the Dharma and the Sangha.
Train in the precepts.
This is good.

THERĪ-GĀTHĀ 246–249

56.

One who grasps the view that the Tathāgata exists,
Having seized the Buddha,
Constructs conceptual fabrications
About one who has achieved nirvāṇa.

NĀGĀRJUNA; *MŪLAMADHYAMAKA-KĀRIKĀ XXII, 13*

57.

A layman who has chosen to practice this Dhamma should not indulge in the drinking of intoxicants. He should not drink them nor encourage others to do so, realizing that it leads to madness. Through intoxication foolish people perform evil deeds and cause other heedless people to do likewise. He should avoid intoxication, this occasion for demerit, which stupefies the mind, and is the pleasure of foolish people.

SUTTA NIPĀTA 398–399

58.

There is no evil like hatred,
And no fortitude like patience.

ŚĀNTIDEVA; *BODHICARYĀVATĀRA 6.2*

59.

The king said: 'Venerable Nāgasena, where does wisdom dwell?'

'Nowhere, O king.'

'Then, Sir, there is no such thing as wisdom.'

'Where does the wind dwell, O king?'

'Not anywhere, Sir.'

'So there is no such thing as wind.'

'Well answered, Nāgasena!'

MILINDAPAÑHA 77

60.

A contented mind is always joyful, but joy like this is but religion; the rich and poor alike, having contentment, enjoy perpetual rest.

The ill-contented man, though he be born to heavenly joys, because he is not contented would ever have a mind burned up by the fire of sorrow.

The rich, without contentment, endures the pain of poverty; though poor, if yet he be contented, then he is rich indeed!

FO-SHO-HING-TSAN-KING 2060–2062

61.

And why are we frightened by her motionless skeleton when we see it lying in the cemetery but not afraid now when we see her zombie-like body moving about like a walking corpse controlled by momentary impulses?

ŚĀNTIDEVA; *BODHICARYĀVATĀRA 8.47*

62.

Here, O Śāriputra, form is emptiness and the very emptiness is form; emptiness does not differ from form, form does not differ from emptiness; whatever is form, that is emptiness, whatever is emptiness, that is form, the same is true of feelings, perceptions, impulses and consciousness.

HEART SUTRA

63.

By him who speaks only to help beings,
It was said that all beings
Have arisen from the conception of I
And are enveloped with the conception of mine.

NĀGĀRJUNA; *PRECIOUS GARLAND 27*

The king said: 'Is a man, Nāgasena, who will not be reborn, aware of the fact?'

'Yes, O king.'

'And how does he know it?'

'By the cessation of all that is cause, proximate or remote, of rebirth.'

'Give me an illustration.'

'Suppose a farmer, great king, had ploughed and sown and filled his granary; and then for a period should neither plough nor sow, but live on the stored up grain, or dispose of it in barter, or deal with it as he had need. Would the farmer be aware, great king, that his granary was not getting filled?'

'Yes, he ought to know it.'

'But how?'

'He would know that the cause, proximate and remote, of the filling of the granary had ceased.'

'Just so with the man you spoke of. By the cessation of all that leads to rebirth, he would be conscious of having escaped his liability to it.'

'Well explained, Nāgasena!'

65.

"It is pleasant, it is unpleasant," so people speak in the world; and based upon that arises desire. Having seen the appearing and disappearing of material things a man makes his judgements in the world. Anger, untruth and doubts, these states arise merely because of the existence of this duality. Let a doubter train himself by way of insight to understand these states as taught by the Recluse.

SUTTA NIPĀTA 867–868

66.

If those who are like wanton children
Are by nature prone to injure others,
What point is there in being angry—
Like resenting fire for its heat?

ŚĀNTIDEVA; *BODHICARYĀVATĀRA 6.39*

67.

Though one should live a hundred years, 'twere all in vain,
Did one not see that all that is doth wax and wane;
Instead, 'twere better far to live a single day,
And know that all the world contains doth rise and pass away.

DHAMMAPADA 113

68.

If you students of the Way wish to become Buddhas, you need study no doctrines whatever, but learn only how to avoid seeking for and attaching yourselves to anything.

HUANG PO; *ZEN TEACHING OF HUANG PO*

69.

There is no specifiable difference whatever between nirvāṇa and the everyday world; there is no specifiable difference whatever between the everyday world and nirvāṇa.

NĀGĀRJUNA; *MŪLAMADHYAMAKA-KĀRIKĀ XXV, 19*

70.

Patience is the sprouting of religion, firmness its root, good conduct is the flower, the enlightened heart the boughs and branches, wisdom supreme the entire tree, the "transcendent law" the fruit, its shade protects all living things. Say then! Why would you cut it down?

FO-SHO-HING-TSAN-KING 1100–1101

71.

When one comes to the Essence of Being,
The shining Wisdom of Reality
Illumines all like the cloudless sky.

HUNDRED THOUSAND SONGS OF MILAREPA

72.

And what, monks, is Right View? It is, monks, the knowledge of suffering, the knowledge of the origin of suffering, the knowledge of the cessation of suffering, and the knowledge of the way of practice leading to the cessation of suffering. This is called Right View.

DĪGHA NIKĀYA ii 311–312

73.

Where there is dependence, there is instability, where there is no
dependence, there is no instability, where there is no instability,
there is quietude, where there is quietude, there is no desire, where
there is no desire, there is no coming and going, where there is no
coming or going, there is no birth or death, where there is no birth
or death, there is neither this world nor that world, nor both: that
is the end of sorrow.

UDĀNA 8.4

74.

Fundamentally, the no-thought of the clover and the no-thought of Śākyamuni are the same. They come forth, and their response to circumstances is to give nourishment. No-thought comes forth here as clover, there as Śākyamuni. Single, universal nature appears like this in the world. We identify clover here and Śākyamuni there, and acknowledge that the two are very different indeed. The clover produces pollen for the bees without a thought; Śākyamuni twirls a flower before his assembly without a thought. But clover cannot call a meeting. Śākyamuni cannot metabolize nutrients directly from the soil.

ROBERT AITKEN; *MIND OF CLOVER*

75.

That which has form emerges from that which has no form; that which has no form emerges from that which has form. Therefore the path of supreme spirituality cannot be sought in being and cannot be fathomed in nonbeing; it cannot be lost through movement and cannot be gained through stillness.

MING-CHIAO; *FIVE HOUSES OF ZEN*

76.

This body, bhikkhus, is perishable, consciousness is of a nature to dissolve, and all objects of clinging are impermanent, suffering and subject to change.

ITIVUTTAKA 77

77.

A man born in the world, by proper thought comes to delight in goodness, he recognizes the impermanence of wealth and beauty, and looks upon religion as his best ornament.

FO-SHO-HING-TSAN-KING 1774

78.

So don't be in a hurry and try to push or rush your practice. Do your meditation gently and gradually step by step. In regard to peacefulness, if you become peaceful, then accept it; if you don't become peaceful, then accept that also. That's the nature of the mind. We must find our own practice and persistently keep at it.

AJAHN CHAH; *BODHINYĀNA*

79.

Here he suffers; after death he suffers: the evildoer suffers in both
   places.
He suffers, he is afflicted, seeing the impurity of his own past
   deeds.

Here he rejoices; after death he rejoices: he that has done good
   works rejoices in both places.
He rejoices, he rejoices exceedingly, seeing the purity of his own
   past deeds.

DHAMMAPADA 15–16

80.

To study the Buddha way is to study oneself. To study oneself is to forget oneself. To forget oneself is to be enlightened by the myriad dharmas. To be enlightened by the myriad dharmas is to bring about the dropping away of body and mind of both oneself and others. The traces of enlightenment come to an end, and this traceless enlightenment is continued endlessly.

DŌGEN; *FLOWERS FALL (SHŌBŌGENZŌ GENJŌKŌAN)*

81.

Every single thing arises from the evil mind, sang the Sage. So there
is nothing dangerous in the three worlds other than the mind.

ŚĀNTIDEVA; *BODHICARYĀVATĀRA 5.8*

82.

Most people never realize that all of us here shall one day perish.
But those who do realize that truth settle their quarrels peacefully.

DHAMMAPADA 6

83.

Happy is he who lives contented in solitude, is well-versed in the Doctrine and who has realized it. Happy is he who lives in this world free from ill-will, and is benevolent towards all beings. Happy is he who lives in this world free from passion, has overcome sensual enjoyment, and who has attained mastership over the conceit of "I am." This indeed is the highest happiness.

UDĀNA 2.1

84.

Now there is cure in coolness and calm, but in heat and passion there can be no cure.

MILINDAPAÑHA 76

85.

In whom there dwells no self-deception and no pride,
Whose lust and selfishness are gone, who is desireless,
Whose wrath is put away, whose self hath cool become—
He is a brahmin, he [is] a recluse, he is a monk.

UDĀNA 3.6

86.

He who seeks happiness should withdraw the arrow: his own lamentations, longings and grief. With the arrow withdrawn, unattached, he would attain to peace of mind; and when all sorrow has been transcended he is sorrow-free and has realized Nibbāna.

SUTTA NIPĀTA 592–593

87.

You yourself have no color or form.
If sent you won't go.
If restrained you don't stay.
If looked for you can't be seen.
If grasped for you can't be caught.

*DRINKING THE MOUNTAIN STREAM: SONGS OF
TIBET'S BELOVED SAINT, MILAREPA*

88.

It is not proper to watch other people. This will not help your practice. If you are annoyed, watch the annoyance in your own mind. If others' discipline is bad or they are not good monks, this is not for you to judge. You will not discover wisdom watching others. Monks' discipline is a tool to use for your own meditation. It is not a weapon to use to criticize or find fault. No one can do your practice for you, nor can you do practice for anyone else. Just be mindful of your own doings. This is the way to practice.

AJAHN CHAH; *BODHINYĀNA*

89.

Yet how painfully do men scheme after wealth, difficult to acquire, easy to dissipate, as that which is got in a dream, how can the wise man hoard up (such trash)!

FO-SHO-HING-TSAN-KING 867

90.

[O]nce a Westerner had come to Wat Pah Pong and asked [Ahjahn Chah] if he was an Arhat. Ahjahn Chah told him, your question is a question to be answered. I will answer it like this: I am like a tree in the forest. Birds come to the tree, they sit on its branches and eat its fruit. To the birds the fruit may be sweet or sour or whatever. But the tree doesn't know anything about it. The birds say sweet or they say sour—from the tree's point of view this is just the chattering of the birds.

PAUL BREITER; *VENERABLE FATHER*

91.

"I have children; I have wealth."
These are the empty claims of an unwise man.
If he cannot call himself his own,
How can he then claim children and wealth as his own?

DHAMMAPADA 62

92.

Ill-governed feelings (senses), like the horse, run wild through all the six domains of sense, bringing upon us in the present world unhappiness, and in the next, birth in an evil way.

So, like the horse ill-broken, these land us in the ditch; therefore the wise and prudent man will not allow his senses license.

For these senses (organs of sense) are, indeed, our greatest foes, causes of misery; for men enamored thus by sensuous things cause all their miseries to recur.

FO-SHO-HING-TSAN-KING 2029–2031

93.

Renunciation is realizing that nostalgia for saṃsāra is full of shit.

CHÖGYAM TRUNGPA; QUOTED IN *WISDOM OF NO ESCAPE*

94.

When people of the world hear it said that the Buddhas transmit the Doctrine of the Mind, they suppose that there is something to be attained or realized apart from Mind, and thereupon they use Mind to seek the Dharma, not knowing that Mind and the object of their search are one.

HUANG PO; *ZEN TEACHING OF HUANG PO*

95.

The victorious ones have said
That emptiness is the relinquishing of all views.
For whomever emptiness is a view,
That one will accomplish nothing.

NĀGĀRJUNA; *MŪLAMADHYAMAKA-KĀRIKĀ XIII, 8*

96.

Herein, Bāhiya, you should train yourself thus: 'In the seen will be merely what is seen; in the heard will be merely what is heard; in the sensed will be merely what is sensed; in the cognized will be merely what is cognized.' In this way you should train yourself, . . . then, Bāhiya, you will not be 'with that'; when, Bāhiya, you are not 'with that,' then, Bāhiya, you will not be 'in that'; when, Bāhiya, you are not 'in that,' then, Bāhiya, you will be neither here nor beyond nor in between the two. Just this is the end of suffering.

UDĀNA 1.10

97.

[T]here is no sweet companion like pure charity.

FO-SHO-HING-TSAN-KING 1508

98.

'[I]t is like the fire which a man, in the cold season, might kindle, and when he had warmed himself, leave still burning, and go away. Then if that fire were to set another man's field on fire, and the owner of the field were to seize him, and bring him before the king, and charge him with the injury, and he were to say: "Your Majesty! It was not I who set this man's field on fire. The fire I left burning was a different one from that which burnt his field. I am not guilty." Now would the man, O king, be guilty?'

'Certainly, Sir.'

'But why?'

'Because, in spite of whatever he might say, he would be guilty in respect of the subsequent fire that resulted from the previous one.'

'Just so, great king, deeds good or evil are done by this name-and-form and another is reborn. But that other is not thereby released from its deeds (its Karma).'

MILINDAPAÑHA 47

99.

The Buddhas of all times and the Zen masters throughout history carry forth the whole earth and hide it in the earth; they smash open the world and take out the world.

DŌGEN; *RATIONAL ZEN*

100.

And what, monks, is Right Thought? The thought of renunciation, the thought of non-ill-will, the thought of harmlessness. This, monks, is called Right Thought.

DĪGHA NIKĀYA ii 312

101.

Buddha-nature is non-duality.

THE SUTRA OF HUI NENG

102.

The king said: 'Your people [Buddhists] say, Nāgasena, that though a man should have lived a hundred years an evil life, yet if, at the moment of death, thoughts of the Buddha should enter his mind, he will be reborn among the gods. This I don't believe. And thus do they also say: "By one case of destruction of life a man may be reborn in purgatory." That, too, I cannot believe.'

'But tell me, O king. Would even a tiny stone float on the water without a boat?'

'Certainly not.'

'Very well; but would not a hundred cart-loads of stones float on the water if they were loaded in a boat?'

'Yes, they would float right enough.'

'Well, good deeds are like the boat.'

'Very good, Nāgasena!'

MILINDAPAÑHA 80

103.

Everything from the smallest kind of happiness up to Buddha-hood comes from sentient beings. All happiness is determined by the activities you do in relation to sentient beings.

SERMEY GESHE LOBSANG THARCHIN; *ESSENCE OF MAHAYANA LOJONG PRACTICE*

104.

The charitable man discarding earthly wealth, nobly excludes the power of covetous desire.

Loving and compassionate now, he gives with reverence and banishes all hatred, envy, anger. So plainly may we see the fruit of charity, putting away all covetous and unbelieving ways.

The bands of sorrow all destroyed, this is the fruit of kindly charity. Know then! The charitable man has found the cause of final rescue.

Even as the man who plants the sapling, thereby secures the shade, the flowers, the fruit (of the tree full grown); the result of charity is even so, its reward is joy and the great Nirvāṇa.

FO-SHO-HING-TSAN-KING 1512–1515

105.

Meditation is like a single log of wood. Insight and investigation are one end of the log; calm and concentration are the other end. If you lift up the whole log, both sides come up at once. Which is concentration and which is insight? Just this mind.

AJAHN CHAH; *STILL FOREST POOL*

106.

Clinging to sense pleasures, to sensual ties,
Seeing in fetters nothing to be blamed,
Never will those tied down by fetters
Cross the flood so wide and great.

UDĀNA 7.3

107.

'Lord, how should we act towards women?' 'Do not see them, Ānanda.' 'But if we see them, how should we behave, Lord?' 'Do not speak to them, Ānanda.' 'But if they speak to us, Lord, how should we behave?' 'Practice mindfulness, Ānanda.'

DĪGHA NIKĀYA ii 141

108.

That very seeing does not see
Itself at all.
How can something that cannot see itself
See another?

NĀGĀRJUNA; *MŪLAMADHYAMAKA-KĀRIKĀ III, 2*

109.

Practice then the art of "giving up" all search[ing]; for "giving up" desire is the joy of perfect rest (Nirvāṇa).

FO-SHO-HING-TSAN-KING 1442

110.

Enemies such as greed and hate lack hands and feet and other limbs.
They are not brave, nor are they wise. How is it they enslave me?

Lodged within my own mind, it is me that they strike down, themselves unshaken. Yet I do not boil with rage at this. Oh, such ill-
placed forbearance!

ŚĀNTIDEVA; *BODHICARYĀVATĀRA 4.28–4.29*

III.

Therefore the practice is like a key, the key of meditation. If we have the right key in our hand, no matter how tightly the lock is closed, when we take the key and turn it the lock falls open. If we have no key we can't open the lock. We will never know what is in the trunk.

AJAHN CHAH; *LIVING DHAMMA*

112.

What the great Buddha has praised as pure, the state that is called immediate, there exists nothing equal to that state.

SUTTA NIPĀTA 226

113.

If you think, "I breathe," the "I" is extra. There is no you to say "I." What we call "I" is just a swinging door which moves when we inhale and when we exhale. It just moves; that is all. When your mind is pure and calm enough to follow this movement, there is nothing: no "I," no world, no mind nor body; just a swinging door.

SHUNRYU SUZUKI; *ZEN MIND, BEGINNER'S MIND*

114.

The mind, indeed, is never seen by any one,
And therefore, whether it can know or cannot know itself,
Just like the beauty of a barren woman's daughter,
This merely forms the subject of a pointless conversation.

ŚĀNTIDEVA; *BODHICARYĀVATĀRA 9.22*

115.

He who treads the Path in earnest
Sees not the mistakes of the world;
If we find fault with others
We ourselves are also in the wrong.

THE SUTRA OF HUI NENG

116.

The king said: 'What is the distinction, Nāgasena, between him who is full of passion, and him who is void of passion?'

'The one is overpowered by craving, O king, and the other not.'

'But what does that mean?'

'The one is in want, O king, and the other not.'

'I look at it, Sir, in this way. He who has passion and he who has not—both of them alike—desire what is good to eat, either hard or soft. And neither of them desires what is wrong.'

'The lustful man, O king, in eating his food enjoys both the taste and the lust that arises from taste, but the man free from lusts experiences the taste only, and not the lust arising therefrom.'

'Well answered, Nāgasena!'

MILINDAPAÑHA 76–77

117.

Not associating with fools, but associating with the wise, and honoring those who deserve honor—this is supreme good fortune.

SUTTA NIPĀTA 259

118.

Have you ever seen flowing water? . . . Have you ever seen still water? . . . If your mind is peaceful it will be just like still, flowing water. Have you ever seen still, flowing water? There! You've only ever seen flowing water and still water, haven't you? But you've never seen still, flowing water. Right there, right where your thinking cannot take you, even though it's peaceful you can develop wisdom. Your mind will be like flowing water, and yet it's still. It's almost as if it were still, and yet it's flowing. So I call it 'still, flowing water'. Wisdom can arise here.

AJAHN CHAH; *LIVING DHAMMA*

119.

By giving, merit grows, by restraint, hatred's checked.
He who's skilled abandons evil things.
As greed, hate and folly wane, Nibbāna's gained.

DĪGHA NIKĀYA ii 136

120.

So much fear and desire come from that commitment to 'I am'—
to being somebody. Eventually they take us to anxiety and despair;
life seems much more difficult and painful than it really is.

But when we just observe life for what it is, then it's all right: the
delights, the beauty, the pleasures, are *just that*. The pain, the dis-
comfort, the sickness, are what they are. We can always cope with
the way life moves and changes. The mind of an enlightened human being is flexible and adaptable. The mind of the ignorant person is conditioned and fixed.

AJAHN SUMEDHO; *SEEING THE WAY*

121.

Although he recites many sacred texts, if he does not act accordingly, that heedless man is like a cowherd who only counts the cattle of others—he does not partake of the blessings of a holy life.

Although he recites few sacred texts, if he puts the Dhamma into practice, forsaking lust, hatred, and delusion, with true wisdom and emancipated mind, clinging to nothing in this or any other world—he, indeed, partakes of the blessings of a holy life.

DHAMMAPADA 19–20

122.

Men are afraid to forget their minds, fearing to fall through the Void with nothing to stay their fall. They do not know that the Void is not really void, but the realm of the real Dharma.

HUANG PO; *ZEN TEACHING OF HUANG PO*

123.

Just as a mother would protect with her life her own son, her only son, so one should cultivate an unbounded mind towards all beings,

and loving-kindness towards all the world. One should cultivate an unbounded mind, above and below and across, without obstruction, without enmity, without rivalry.

Standing, or going, or seated, or lying down, as long as one is free from drowsiness, one should practice this mindfulness. This, they say, is the holy state here.

SUTTA NIPĀTA 149–151

124.

Like covering over with a false surface a hole full of fire, slipping thro' which the body is burnt, so is the fire of covetous desire. The wise man meddles not with it.

FO-SHO-HING-TSAN-KING 868

125.

Feelings, whether of compassion or irritation, should be welcomed, recognized, and treated on an absolutely equal basis; because both are ourselves. The tangerine I am eating is me. The mustard greens I am planting are me. I plant with all my heart and mind. I clean this teapot with the kind of attention I would have were I giving the baby Buddha or Jesus a bath. Nothing should be treated more carefully than anything else. In mindfulness, compassion, irritation, mustard green plant, and teapot are all sacred.

THICH NHAT HANH; *MIRACLE OF MINDFULNESS!*

126.

Disastrous, bhikkhus, are gain, honor and fame, a bitter, severe danger to the attainment of unsurpassed security from bondage. Therefore, bhikkhus, you should train yourselves thus:

'When gain, honor and fame have arisen we will renounce them and will not let them establish a hold over our hearts.'

SAMYUTTA NIKĀYA XVII. 1, 1

127.

Do not choose bad friends.
Do not choose persons of low habits.
Select good friends. Be discriminating.
Choose the best.

DHAMMAPADA 78

128.

Actually this practice is just about the mind and its feelings. It's not something that you have to run after or struggle for. Breathing continues while working. Nature takes care of the natural processes—all we have to do is try to be aware. Just to keep trying, going inwards to see clearly. Meditation is like this.

AJAHN CHAH; *TASTE OF FREEDOM*

129.

By realizing that all forms are self-awareness,
I have beheld my consort's face—the true Mind Within.

HUNDRED THOUSAND SONGS OF MILAREPA

130.

Now suppose a cowherd wanted to tame a wild calf that had been reared on a wild cow's milk, he would take it away from the cow and tie it up apart with a rope to a stout post dug into the ground; then the calf might dash to and fro, but being unable to get away, it would eventually sit down or lie down by the post, so too, when a bhikkhu wants to tame his own mind which has long been spoilt by being reared on visible data, etc., as object for its food and drink, he should take it away from visible data, etc., as object and bring it into the forest or to the root of a tree or to an empty place and tie it up there to the post of in-breaths and out-breaths with the rope of mindfulness. And so his mind may then dash to and fro when it no longer gets the objects it was formerly used to, but being unable to break the rope of mindfulness and get away, it sits down, lies down, by that object under the influence of access and absorption.

BUDDHAGHOSA; *VISUDDHIMAGGA 268–269*

131.

I now will seek (he said) a noble law, unlike the worldly methods
known to men, I will oppose disease and age and death, and strive
against the mischief wrought by these on men.

FO-SHO-HING-TSAN-KING 339

132.

One sees pleasure as suffering
And sees pain as a dart.
One sees as impermanent the peaceful feeling
That is neither pleasant nor painful.

Such a bhikkhu who sees rightly
Is thereby well released.
Accomplished in knowledge, at peace,
That sage has overcome all bonds.

ITIVUTTAKA 53

133.

[T]he want of faith (doubt) is the engulfing sea, the presence of disorderly belief is the rolling flood,

The tide of lust carries away the world; involved in its eddies there is no escape; wisdom is the handy boat, reflection is the hold-fast.

FO-SHO-HING-TSAN-KING 1664–1665

134.

He who knows that his body is like foam, he who clearly compre-
hends that it is of the nature of a mirage,
Such a man will break the flower-tipped arrows of Māra and will
go where the King of Death will not see him.

DHAMMAPADA 46

135.

Without realizing the unity of Bliss and Void,
Even though on the Void you meditate,
You practice only Nihilism.

HUNDRED THOUSAND SONGS OF MILAREPA

136.

Crookedness and truth (straightness) are in their nature opposite and cannot dwell together more than frost and fire; for one who has become religious, and practices the way of straight behavior, a false and crooked way of speech is not becoming.

FO-SHO-HING-TSAN-KING 2055

137.

Even if you are a monk, if your practice of the Way is not intense, if your aspiration is not pure, how are you any different from a layman? Again, even if you are a layman, if your aspiration is intense and your conduct wise, why is this any different from being a monk?

HAKUIN; *ZEN MASTER HAKUIN*

138.

Having drunk the sweetness of solitude and also the sweetness of tranquility, one becomes free from fear and wrongdoing while drinking the sweetness of the joy of truth.

SUTTA NIPĀTA 257

139.

[The] defilements are like a cat. If you feed it, it will keep coming around. Stop feeding it, and eventually it will not bother to come around any more.

AJAHN CHAH; *STILL FOREST POOL*

140.

We who are like senseless children
Shrink from suffering, but love its causes.
We hurt ourselves; our pain is self-inflicted!
Why should *others* be the object of our anger?

ŚĀNTIDEVA; *BODHICARYĀVATĀRA 6.45*

141.

You and I come forth as possibilities of essential nature, alone and independent as stars, yet reflecting and being reflected by all things. My life and yours are the unfolding realization of total aloneness and total intimacy. The self is completely autonomous, yet exists only in resonance with all other selves.

ROBERT AITKEN; *MIND OF CLOVER*

142.

The lily growing on the tranquil lake, in its midst harbors count-less noisome insects; and so the towering abode of the rich is the house of calamity; the wise will not dwell therein.

FO-SHO-HING-TSAN-KING 719

143.

"We Samanas seek release from the Self, O Illustrious One. If I were one of your followers, I fear that it would only be on the surface, that I would deceive myself that I was at peace and had attained salvation, while in truth the Self would continue to live and grow, for it would have been transformed into your teachings, into my allegiance and love for you and for the community of the monks."

Half smiling, with imperturbable brightness and friendliness, the Buddha looked steadily at the stranger and dismissed him with a hardly visible gesture.

"You are clever, O Samana," said the Illustrious One, "you know how to speak cleverly, my friend. Be on your guard against too much cleverness."

The Buddha walked away and his look and half-smile remained imprinted on Siddhartha's memory forever.

HERMANN HESSE; *SIDDHARTHA*

144.

One who studies and doesn't practice is like a ladle in a soup pot. It's in the pot every day but it doesn't know the flavor of the soup. If you don't practice, even if you study till the day you die, you won't know the taste of freedom!

AJAHN CHAH; *TASTE OF FREEDOM*

145.

To meditate means to realize inwardly the imperturbability of the
Essence of Mind.

THE SUTRA OF HUI NENG

146.

When you observe your mind with penetration,
Stir not ardent passion or attachment
Lest the devil of desire possess you.
Son, rest at ease and without hope.

HUNDRED THOUSAND SONGS OF MILAREPA

147.

Whatever harm an enemy may do to an enemy, or a hater to a hater, an ill-directed mind inflicts on oneself greater harm.

DHAMMAPADA 42

148.

At first they are called stopping and seeing, to help new learners; later they become concentration and wisdom, roots of enlightenment.

These are only one reality, which seems to have two parts.

YUNG-MING; *FIVE HOUSES OF ZEN*

149.

It is not that I am careless about beauty, or am ignorant of (the power of) human joys, but only that I see on all the impress of change; therefore my heart is sad and heavy;

If these things were sure of lasting, without the ills of age, disease, and death, then would I too take my fill of love; and to the end find no disgust or sadness. . . .

FO-SHO-HING-TSAN-KING 302–303

150.

So, when a fool does wrong deeds, he does not realize (their evil nature); by his own deeds the stupid man is tormented, like one burnt by fire.

DHAMMAPADA 136

151.

According to the Buddhist tradition, the spiritual path is the process of cutting through our confusion, of uncovering the awakened state of mind. When the awakened state of mind is crowded in by ego and its attendant paranoia, it takes on the character of an underlying instinct. So it is not a matter of building up the awakened state of mind, but rather of burning out the confusions which obstruct it. In the process of burning out these confusions, we discover enlightenment. If the process were otherwise, the awakened state of mind would be a product, dependent upon cause and effect and therefore liable to dissolution.

CHÖGYAM TRUNGPA; *CUTTING THROUGH*
SPIRITUAL MATERIALISM

152.

When the ear hears, observe the mind. Does it get caught up and make a story out of the sound? Is it disturbed? You can know this, stay with it, be aware. At times you may want to escape from the sound, but that is not the way out. You must escape through awareness.

AJAHN CHAH; *STILL FOREST POOL*

153.

When there is grasping, the grasper
Comes into existence.
If he did not grasp,
Then being freed, he would not come into existence.

NĀGĀRJUNA; *MŪLAMADHYAMAKA-KĀRIKĀ XXVI*, 7

154.

Victory produces hatred; he that is defeated is afflicted with
   suffering;
He that has renounced both victory and defeat lives in tranquillity and happiness.

DHAMMAPADA 201

155.

If you only believe that Buddha speaks no words,
Then the Lotus will blossom in your mouth.

THE SUTRA OF HUI NENG

156.

It is suffering that exists,
suffering that endures,
suffering that disappears.

Nothing but suffering exists.
Nothing but suffering comes to an end.

SAṂYUTTA NIKĀYA V. 10

157.

Bhikkhus, if beings knew, as I know, the result of giving and sharing, they would not eat without having given nor would they allow the stain of meanness to obsess them and take root in their minds. Even if it were their last morsel, their last mouthful, they would not enjoy eating without having shared it, if there were someone to share it with.

ITIVUTTAKA 26

158.

Each individual must personally realize true happiness through the eradication of the mind's defilements. As suffering is born within one's own mind, it must be overcome within one's own mind. None can impart freedom from suffering to another. To accomplish this aim one first has to understand suffering and its cause, and then . . . develop the path leading to release. Insight meditation, or *vipassanā-bhāvanā*, is the plan of action culminating in final liberation. Apart from the development of insight there is no other way to deliverance from suffering.

MĀTARA ŚRI ÑĀṆĀRĀMA;
SEVEN CONTEMPLATIONS OF INSIGHT

159.

As sweet as honey, thinks a fool an evil deed, so long as it bears
    no fruit;
But when it bears fruit, then the fool comes to grief.

DHAMMAPADA 69

160.

If anyone whose mind is not harmonized and controlled through methodical meditative training should take a close look at his own everyday thoughts and activities, he will meet with a rather disconcerting sight. Apart from the few main channels of his purposeful thoughts and activities, he will everywhere be faced with a tangled mass of perceptions, thoughts, feelings, and casual bodily movements showing a disorderliness and confusion which he would certainly not tolerate in his living-room. Yet this is the state of affairs that we take for granted within a considerable portion of our waking life and our normal mental activity.

NYANAPONIKA THERA; *POWER OF MINDFULNESS*

161.

For there is suffering, but none who suffers;
Doing exists although there is no doer;
Extinction is but no extinguished person;
Although there is a path, there is no goer.

BUDDHAGHOSA; *VISUDDHIMAGGA 513*

162.

If resistance to meditation is a common feature of your practice, then you should suspect some subtle error in your basic attitude. Meditation is not a ritual conducted in a particular posture. It is not a painful exercise, or period of enforced boredom. And it is not a grim, solemn obligation. Meditation is mindfulness. It is a new way of seeing and it is a form of play. Meditation is your friend. Come to regard it as such and resistance will disappear like smoke on a summer breeze.

HENEPOLA GUNARATANA; *MINDFULNESS IN PLAIN ENGLISH*

163.

[E]vil words will be repeated far and wide by the multitude, but there are few to follow good direction. . . .

FO-SHO-HING-TSAN-KING 1640

164.

A person getting enlightened is like the moon reflecting in the water. The moon does not get wet, the water is not disturbed. Though it is a great expanse of light, it reflects in a little bit of water; the whole moon and the whole sky reflect even in the dew on the grass; they reflect even in a single drop of water. Enlightenment not disturbing the person is like the moon not piercing the water. A person not obstructing enlightenment is like the dewdrop not obstructing the heavens.

DŌGEN; *FLOWERS FALL (SHŌBŌGENZŌ GENJŌKŌAN)*

165.

Just as deer and birds caught in the hunter's snare will eventually be killed, under the influence of delusion beings are enmeshed in the net of saṃsāra. Don't you see that in the past all beings have been devoured by the Lord of Death and that you too will come to the same end? Regardless of their age, health or any other consideration, the Lord of Death is systematically slaughtering all those around you. If you realize this, why don't you practice the dharma instead of pursuing worldly desires and indulging in sleep? You are like the buffalo who stupidly continues to eat his grass unconcerned that all around him are being taken to slaughter.

ŚĀNTIDEVA; *BODHICARYĀVATĀRA 7.4–7.6*

166.

The fool who thinks he is a fool is for that very reason a wise
    man;
But the fool who thinks he is a wise man is rightly called a fool.

DHAMMAPADA 63

167.

Wisdom is but Self-awareness,
Beyond all words and talk!

HUNDRED THOUSAND SONGS OF MILAREPA

168.

From pure behavior comes self-power, which frees a man from (many) dangers; pure conduct, like a ladder, enables us to climb to heaven.

FO-SHO-HING-TSAN-KING 1806

169.

We may shout, "Let there be peace!" but this won't really bring peace. Peace will appear in the world around us only when each individual learns to tame the disturbances arising within his or her own mind. Then, peace will come automatically.

CHÖKYI NYIMA RINPOCHE; *UNION OF MAHAMUDRA AND DZOGCHEN*

170.

O you who wish to guard your minds,
I beseech you with folded hands;
Always exert yourselves to guard
Mindfulness and alertness!

People who are disturbed by sickness
Have no strength to do anything (useful),
Likewise those whose minds are disturbed by confusion
Have no strength to do anything (wholesome).

ŚĀNTIDEVA; *BODHICARYĀVATĀRA* 5.23–5.24

171.

For one road leads to [worldly] gain, the other to Nibbāna.
Understanding this, the monk, the disciple of the Buddha,
Should not delight in worldly gain, but should devote himself to
  solitude.

DHAMMAPADA 75

172.

Traditionally the Eightfold Path is taught with eight steps such as Right Understanding, Right Speech, Right Concentration, and so forth. But the true Eightfold Path is within us—two eyes, two ears, two nostrils, a tongue, and a body. These eight doors are our entire Path and the mind is the one that walks on the Path. Know these doors, examine them, and all the dharmas will be revealed.

AJAHN CHAH; *STILL FOREST POOL*

173.

The king said: 'By what, Nāgasena, does one recollect what is past and done long ago?'

'By memory.'

'But is it not by the mind, [rather than] by the memory, that we recollect?'

'Do you recollect any business, O king, that you have done and then forgotten?'

'Yes.'

'What then? Were you then without a mind?'

'No. But my memory failed me.'

'Then why do you say that it is by the mind, not by the memory, that we recollect?'

'Very good, Nāgasena!'

MILINDAPAÑHA 77

174.

Take no pleasure in worldly talk;
Take delight in what passes beyond the world.
Cause good qualities to grow in others
In the same way (you wish them) for yourself.

NĀGĀRJUNA; *PRECIOUS GARLAND 266*

175.

Right meditation is not escapism; it is not meant to provide hiding-places for temporary oblivion. Realistic meditation has the purpose of training the mind to face, to understand and to conquer this very world in which we live.

NYANAPONIKA THERA; *POWER OF MINDFULNESS*

176.

He who has burned out his evil thoughts,
entirely cut them off within his heart,
—such a monk gives up the here and the beyond,
just as a serpent sheds its worn-out skin.

SUTTA NIPĀTA 7

177.

The action of subject and object are all dissolved in the sphere of
   the clear light,
By definitely knowing that causation is emptiness.
Then the subject and object are eliminated.

HUNDRED THOUSAND SONGS: SELECTIONS FROM MILAREPA,
POET-SAINT OF TIBET

178.

Speak not harshly to anyone. Those thus addressed will retort. Painful, indeed, is vindictive speech. Blows in exchange may bruise you.

If, like a cracked gong, you silence yourself, you have already attained Nibbāna: no vindictiveness will be found in you.

DHAMMAPADA 133–134

179.

Greed, I say, is a great flood; it is a whirlpool sucking one down, a constant yearning, seeking a hold, continually in movement; difficult to cross is the morass of sensual desire. A sage does not deviate from truth, a brāhmaṇa stands on firm ground; renouncing all, he is truly called 'calmed.'

SUTTA NIPĀTA 945–946

180.

Going along in company together, a wise man
Must mix with other foolish persons.
But on seeing what is wrongful he abandons them.
As a full-fledged heron leaves the marshy ground.

UDĀNA 8.7

181.

This fundamental consciousness
In itself is nothing at all.
In the voidness of reality
Lack of realizer and realized is realized,
Lack of seer and seen is seen,
Lack of knower and known is known,
Lack of perceiver and percept is perceived.

*DRINKING THE MOUNTAIN STREAM: SONGS OF
TIBET'S BELOVED SAINT, MILAREPA*

182.

Now you have seen the true doctrine, your guileless heart loves to exercise its charity, for wealth and money are inconstant treasures, 'twere better quickly to bestow such things on others.

FO-SHO-HING-TSAN-KING 1502

183.

Few among men cross over to the further shore; the multitudes who remain run to and fro on this shore.

Those who live according to the Dhamma which has been well proclaimed (by the Buddha) will cross over the impassable realm of death to the further shore.

DHAMMAPADA 85–86

184.

All the harm with which this world is rife,
All fear and suffering that there is,
Clinging to the "I" has caused it!
What am I to do with this great demon?

If this "I" is not relinquished wholly,
Sorrow likewise cannot be avoided.
For if he does not keep away from fire,
A man cannot escape from being burned.

ŚĀNTIDEVA; *BODHICARYĀVATĀRA 8.134–8.135*

185.

Thus shall ye think of all this fleeting world:
A star at dawn, a bubble in a stream;
A flash of lightning in a summer cloud,
A flickering lamp, a phantom, and a dream.

DIAMOND SUTRA

186.

Abandoning harsh speech, he abstains from harsh speech, he speaks such words as are gentle, pleasing to the ear, and lovable, as go to the heart, are courteous, desired by many and agreeable to many.

MAJJHIMA-NIKĀYA i.179

187.

I urge you not to throw away time, for it's swift as an arrow, fast as a stream. Distraction is entirely due to lack of concentration; stupidity and blindness are caused by lack of true knowledge.

YUNG-MING; *FIVE HOUSES OF ZEN*

188.

Some are ashamed of what is not shameful,
And shameless about what is shameful.
Following such false views,
They go to a sorrowful state.

Some are fearful where there is nothing to fear,
And are fearless where there is much to fear.
Holding such false views,
They go to a sorrowful state.

Some see what is right as wrong
And what is wrong as right.
Holding such false views,
They go to a sorrowful state.

Those who see wrong as wrong
And right as right
Hold right views,
And go to a joyful state.

DHAMMAPADA 316–319

189.

Both the young and the old, whether they are foolish or wise, are going to be trapped by death. All beings move towards death.

They are overcome by death. They go to the other world. And then not even a father can save his son, or a family their relatives.

SUTTA NIPĀTA 578–579

190.

For having spewed forth lust, passion, and ignorance, shall I return to feed upon it? As a man might go back to his vomit! Such misery, how could I bear?

FO-SHO-HING-TSAN-KING 727

191.

Neither from itself nor from another,
Nor from both,
Nor without a cause,
Does anything whatever, anywhere arise.

NĀGĀRJUNA; *MŪLAMADHYAMAKA-KĀRIKĀ I, 1*

192.

Then the Lord said to the monks: 'Now, monks, I declare to you: all conditioned things are of a nature to decay—strive on untiringly.' These were the Tathāgata's last words.

DĪGHA NIKĀYA ii 155–156

193.

Mindfulness is the miracle by which we master and restore ourselves. Consider, for example: a magician who cuts his body into
many parts and places each part in a different region—hands in
the south, arms in the east, legs in the north, and then by some
miraculous power lets forth a cry which reassembles whole every
part of his body. Mindfulness is like that—it is the miracle which
can call back in a flash our dispersed mind and restore it to whole-
ness so that we can live each minute of life.

THICH NHAT HANH; *MIRACLE OF MINDFULNESS*

194.

There is no fire like the fire of lust;
There is no sin like the sin of hatred;
There are no sufferings like the sufferings of existence;
There is no happiness like Supreme Tranquillity.

DHAMMAPADA 202

195.

What others call happiness, that the Noble Ones declare to be suffering. What others call suffering, that the Noble Ones have found to be happiness. See how difficult it is to understand the Dhamma! Herein those without insight have completely gone astray.

SUTTA NIPĀTA 762

196.

The fire which fiercely burns the desert grass (dies out), and then the grass will grow again;

But when the fire of lust burns up the heart, then how hard for true religion there to dwell!

FO-SHO-HING-TSAN-KING 1815–1816

197.

Hey you, expecting results without effort! So sensitive! So long-suffering! You, in the clutches of death, acting like an immortal! Hey, sufferer, you are destroying yourself!

ŚĀNTIDEVA; *BODHICARYĀVATĀRA* 7.13

198.

His thoughts are calm, his speech is calm, his deeds are calm;
Such is the calm of one who has obtained Deliverance by Right
Knowledge.

DHAMMAPADA 96

199.

Of slight account, monks, is the loss of such things as reputation. Miserable indeed among losses is the loss of wisdom.

Of slight account, monks, is the increase of such things as reputation. Chief of all the increases is that of wisdom.

ANGUTTARA-NIKĀYA i.15

200.

Fools and reificationists who perceive
The existence and nonexistence
Of objects
Do not see the pacification of objectification.

NĀGĀRJUNA; *MŪLAMADHYAMAKA-KĀRIKĀ V, 8*

201.

Wisdom comes out in the village of infinite nothingness; spirituality is found in the realm of unfathomability. Where dragons and elephants tread is not within the capability of asses.

FA-YEN; *FIVE HOUSES OF ZEN*

202.

So within this mountain-wall of old age, birth, disease, and death, there is no escape for the world. Only by considering and practicing the true law can we escape from this sorrow-piled mountain.

FO-SHO-HING-TSAN-KING 1644

203.

Although wishing to be rid of misery,
They run towards misery itself.
Although wishing to have happiness,
Like an enemy they ignorantly destroy it.

ŚĀNTIDEVA; *BODHICARYĀVATĀRA 1.28*

204.

Though one should conquer a thousand times a thousand men in
   battle,
Yet would he be the mightiest conqueror who should conquer
   one, himself.

DHAMMAPADA 103

205.

I prostrate to Gautama
Who through compassion
Taught the true doctrine,
Which leads to the relinquishing of all views.

NĀGĀRJUNA; *MŪLAMADHYAMAKA-KĀRIKĀ XXVII, 30*

206.

The king said: 'Where there is no transmigration, Nāgasena, can there be rebirth?'

'Yes, there can.'

'But how can that be? Give me an illustration.'

'Suppose a man, O king, were to light a lamp from another lamp, can it be said that the one transmigrates from, or to, the other?'

'Certainly not.'

'Just so, great king, is rebirth without transmigration.'

'Give me a further illustration.'

'Do you recollect, great king, having learnt, when you were a boy, some verse or other from your teacher?'

'Yes, I recollect that.'

'Well then, did that verse transmigrate from your teacher?'

'Certainly not.'

'Just so, great king, is rebirth without transmigration.'

'Very good, Nāgasena!'

MILINDAPAÑHA 71

207.

Those who wish to guard their practice
Should very attentively guard their minds
For those who do not guard their minds
Will be unable to guard their practice.

ŚĀNTIDEVA; *BODHICARYĀVATĀRA 5.1*

208.

If you are happy in meditating on your self-mind,
You should know that disturbing thoughts are a manifestation of
   the mind.
Therefore, identify your self with the mind essence.

HUNDRED THOUSAND SONGS: SELECTIONS FROM

MILAREPA, POET-SAINT OF TIBET

209.

Q: I can observe anger and work with greed, but how does one
   observe delusion?
A: You're riding a horse and asking "Where's the horse?" Pay
   attention.

AJAHN CHAH; *STILL FOREST POOL*

210.

Arise! Sit up!
What advantage is there in your sleeping;
What sleep is there to those who are afflicted by disease,
Pierced by the arrow of suffering?

SUTTA NIPĀTA 331

211.

Have you ever seen a wheat or barley field in late summer? Sometimes, when the crops have grown nicely and the heads of the plants are rich with grain, the tops bend over. The stalks of the plants can't hold those rich heads of grain upright. And when the plant does not produce a full head of grain, it stands very straight as the breeze blows over it. This means that the heads are almost empty. Plants that are empty of grain will naturally stand higher and plants that are rich with grain will bend over. Actually, it is much the same with us.

SERMEY GESHE LOBSANG THARCHIN; *ESSENCE OF MAHAYANA LOJONG PRACTICE*

212.

The real basis of Buddhism is full knowledge of the truth of reality. If one knows this truth then no teaching is necessary. If one doesn't know, even if he listens to the teaching, he doesn't really hear.

AJAHN CHAH; *TASTE OF FREEDOM*

213.

A man was rowing his boat upstream on a very misty morning. Suddenly, he saw another boat coming downstream, not trying to avoid him. It was coming straight at him. He shouted, "Be careful! Be careful!" but the boat came right into him, and his boat was almost sunk. The man became very angry, and began to shout at the other person, to give him a piece of his mind. But when he looked closely, he saw that there was no one in the other boat. It turned out that the boat just got loose and went downstream. All his anger vanished, and he laughed and he laughed.

THICH NHAT NANH; *BEING PEACE*

214.

Nothing is born, nothing is destroyed. Away with your dualism, your likes and dislikes. Every single thing is just the One Mind. When you have perceived this, you will have mounted the Chariot of the Buddhas.

HUANG PO; *ZEN TEACHING OF HUANG PO*

215.

By self alone is evil done, by self alone does one suffer.
By self alone is evil left undone, by self alone does one obtain
Salvation.
Salvation and Perdition depend upon self; no man can save
another.

DHAMMAPADA 165

216.

I prostrate to the Perfect Buddha,
The best of teachers, who taught that
Whatever is dependently arisen is
Unceasing, unborn,
Unannihilated, not permanent,
Not coming, not going,
Without distinction, without identity,
And free from conceptual construction.

NĀGĀRJUNA; *MŪLAMADHYAMAKA-KĀRIKĀ*

DEDICATORY VERSES

217.

Abandoning false speech, he abstains from false speech; he speaks truth, adheres to truth, is trustworthy and reliable, one who is no deceiver of the world.

MAJJHIMA-NIKĀYA i.179

218.

By realizing the true nature of the mind,

The Yogin sees the clear light, [which] neither comes nor goes.

The appearance of the external world is an illusion.

By observation of the nature of manifestations,

He realizes the identity of manifestations and void,

And by understanding, he knows the two are not different.

HUNDRED THOUSAND SONGS: SELECTIONS FROM

MILAREPA, POET-SAINT OF TIBET

219.

Through many a birth I wandered in saṃsāra, seeking, but not finding, the builder of the house. Sorrowful is it to be born again and again.

O house-builder! Thou art seen. Thou shalt build no house again. All thy rafters are broken. Thy ridge-pole is shattered.

My mind has attained the unconditioned. Achieved is the end of craving.

DHAMMAPADA 153–154

220.

Your evil thoughts and evil words but hurt yourself and not another; nothing so full of victory as patience, though your body suffer the pain of mutilation.

FO-SHO-HING-TSAN-KING 2047

221.

Tung-shan asked a monk, "Where have you come from?"

The monk replied, "From a journey to a mountain."

Tung-shan asked, "And did you reach the peak?"

The monk said, "Yes."

Tung-shan asked, "Was there anyone on the peak?"

The monk answered, "No."

Tung-shan said, "Then you didn't reach the peak."

The monk retorted, "If I didn't reach the peak, how could I know there was no one there?"

Tung-shan said, "I had doubted this fellow."

TUNG-SHAN; *FIVE HOUSES OF ZEN*

222.

[P]assion is the cause of blindness, of not seeing, of not knowing, of loss of insight: it is joined with vexation, it does not conduce to Nibbāna.

ANGUTTARA-NIKĀYA i.216

223.

[Aranyabho] had a sheepish grin on his face as Ahjahn Chah was good naturedly berating him. As I sat down Ahjahn Chah said, "Aranyabho's got dogshit in his pocket." I didn't say anything, waiting for the explanation. "Aranyabho's got dogshit in his pocket. He goes somewhere and sits down but there's a bad smell, so he thinks, hmmm, this place is no good. He gets up and goes somewhere else, but he notices the bad smell again so then he goes somewhere else. . . . He doesn't realize he's carrying the dogshit around with him wherever he goes. . . ."

PAUL BREITER; *VENERABLE FATHER*

224.

All is empty! Neither "self," nor place for "self," but all the world is like a phantasy; this is the way to regard ourselves, as but a heap of composite qualities (saṃskāra).

FO-SHO-HING-TSAN-KING 1449

225.

For consider the world—
A bubble, a mirage.
See the world as it is,
And death shall overlook you.

Come, consider the world,
A painted chariot for kings,
A trap for fools.
But he who sees goes free.

DHAMMAPADA 170–171

226.

We say, "In calmness there should be activity; in activity there should be calmness." Actually, they are the same thing; to say "calmness" or to say "activity" is just to express two different interpretations of one fact. There is harmony in our activity, and where there is harmony there is calmness. This harmony is the quality of being. But the quality of being is also nothing but its speedy activity.

SHUNRYU SUZUKI; *ZEN MIND, BEGINNER'S MIND*

227.

'When wisdom springs up in the heart, O king, it dispels the darkness of ignorance, it causes the radiance of knowledge to arise, it makes the light of intelligence to shine forth, and it makes the Noble Truths plain. Thus does the recluse who is devoted to effort perceive with the clearest wisdom the impermanency (of all beings and things). The suffering (that is inherent in individuality), and the absence of any soul.'

'Give me an illustration.'

'It is like a lamp, O king, which a man might introduce into a house in darkness. When the lamp had been brought in it would dispel the darkness, cause radiance to arise, and light to shine forth, and make the objects there plainly visible. Just so would wisdom in a man have such effects as were just now set forth.'

'Well put, Nāgasena!'

MILINDAPAÑHA 39

228.

Though in thought we range throughout the world,
We'll nowhere find a thing more dear than self.
So, since others hold the self so dear,
He who loves himself should injure none.

SAMYUTTA NIKĀYA III. 1, 8

229.

[A]ll manifestations (consist in) Mind, and Mind is the Illuminating-
Voidness without any shadow or impediment.

HUNDRED THOUSAND SONGS OF MILAREPA

230.

The Lord taught a holy life
Not based on tradition,
For restraint and abandoning,
Leading to and merging in Nibbāna.

This is the path followed by the great,
Pursued by the lofty sages.
Those who enter that course
As taught by the Enlightened One,
Heeding the Teacher's instruction,
Will make an end of suffering.

ITIVUTTAKA 35

231.

Irrigators regulate the waters; arrow-makers straighten arrow shafts; carpenters shape wood; and the good control themselves.

DHAMMAPADA 145

232.

Life has no whence; it is carrying forth, and carrying forth again.
Death has no whither; it is carrying away, and carrying away
again.

Ultimately how is it?

If the mind does not differ, myriad things are one suchness.

DŌGEN; *RATIONAL ZEN*

233.

Hey! Listen all you gathered here—
View mind and body in this way:
Mind is insubstantial, void awareness,
Body a bubble of flesh and blood.

DRINKING THE MOUNTAIN STREAM: SONGS OF
TIBET'S BELOVED SAINT, MILAREPA

The king said: 'Why is it, Nāgasena, that all men are not alike, but some are short-lived and some long-lived, some sickly and some healthy, some ugly and some beautiful, some without influence and some of great power, some poor and some wealthy, some low born and some high born, some stupid and some wise?'

The Elder replied: 'Why is it that all vegetables are not alike, but some sour, and some salt, and some pungent, and some acid, and some astringent, and some sweet?'

'I fancy, Sir, it is because they come from different kinds of seeds.'

'And just so, great king, are the differences you have mentioned among men to be explained. For it has been said by the Blessed One: "Beings, O brahmin, have each their own Karma, are inheritors of Karma, belong to the tribe of their Karma, are relatives by Karma, have each their Karma as their protecting overlord. It is Karma that divides them up into low and high and the like divisions."'

'Very good, Nāgasena!'

MILINDAPAÑHA 65

235.

The dharma that is taught and the dharma that is experienced are descriptions of how to live, how to use your life to wake you up rather than put you to sleep. And if you choose to spend the rest of your life trying to find out what awake means and what asleep means, I think you might attain enlightenment.

PEMA CHÖDRÖN; *WISDOM OF NO ESCAPE*

236.

The perceiving of impermanence, bhikkhus, developed and frequently practiced, removes all sensual passion, removes all passion for material existence, removes all passion for becoming, removes all ignorance, removes and abolishes all conceit of 'I am.'

Just as in the autumn a farmer, ploughing with a large plough cuts through all the spreading rootlets as he ploughs; in the same way, bhikkhus, the perceiving of impermanence, developed and frequently practiced, removes all sensual passion . . . removes and abolishes all conceit of 'I am.'

SAṂYUTTA NIKĀYA XXII. 102

237.

Long is the night to the wakeful; long is the league to the weary;
long is saṃsāra to the foolish who know not the Sublime Truth.

DHAMMAPADA 60

238.

There are, bhikkhus, two successive Dhamma-teachings of the Tathāgata, the Arahant, the Fully Enlightened One. What are the two?
'See evil as evil'—this is the first Dhamma-teaching. 'Having seen
evil as evil, be rid of it, be detached from it, be freed from it'—this
is the second Dhamma-teaching.

ITIVUTTAKA 39

239.

The defining characteristic of guarding alertness
In brief is only this:
To examine again and again
The condition of my body and mind.

Therefore I shall put this way of life into actual practice,
For what can be achieved by merely talking about it?
Will a sick man be benefited
Merely by reading the medical texts?

ŚĀNTIDEVA; *BODHICARYĀVATĀRA 5.108–5.109*

240.

Eh ma! All things of saṃsāra and nirvāṇa
Don't exist—yet appear—
Appear—yet are void—why?

DRINKING THE MOUNTAIN STREAM: SONGS OF TIBET'S BELOVED SAINT, MILAREPA

The king said: 'You were talking just now of name-and-form. What does "name" mean in that expression, and what "form"?'

'Whatever is gross therein, that is "form": whatever is subtle, mental, that is "name."'

'Why is it, Nāgasena, that name is not reborn separately, or form separately?'

'These conditions, great king, are connected one with the other, and spring into being together.'

'Give me an illustration.'

'As a hen, great king, would not get a yoke or an egg-shell separately, but both would arise in one, they two being intimately dependent one on the other; just so, if there were no name there would be no form. What is meant by name in that expression being intimately dependent on what is meant by form, they spring up together. And this is, through time immemorial, their nature.'

MILINDAPAÑHA 49

242.

Considering the harm others do to you
As created by your former deeds, do not anger.
Act such that further suffering will not be created
And your own faults will disappear.

NĀGĀRJUNA; *PRECIOUS GARLAND 271*

243.

He who entirely cuts off his craving
by drying up its fierce and rapid flow,
—such a monk gives up the here and the beyond,
just as a serpent sheds its worn-out skin.

SUTTA NIPĀTA 3

244.

Monks, there are these three roots of evil. What three?

Lust is a root of evil, hate is a root of evil, delusion is a root of evil. These are the three roots of evil.

ITIVUTTAKA 50

245.

When a tree is burning with fierce flames how can the birds congregate therein? The wise man, who is regarded as an enlightened sage, without this knowledge is ignorant;

Having this knowledge, then true wisdom dawns; without it, there is no enlightenment. To get this wisdom is the one aim, to neglect it is the mistake of life.

FO-SHO-HING-TSAN-KING 1659–1660

246.

Saṃsāra in itself is groundless and unreal;
When you look you find it hard
To define, ungraspable.
Yet when you realize it,
It is Nirvāṇa itself.
All things in themselves are void;
A yogi is attached to nothing.

HUNDRED THOUSAND SONGS OF MILAREPA

247.

He who realizes the Essence of Mind within himself
Knows that the 'True Mind' is to be sought apart from
    phenomena.
If one's mind is bound by illusive phenomena
Where is Reality to be found, when all phenomena are unreal?

THE SUTRA OF HUI NENG

248.

Do not think lightly of evil, saying, "It will not come to me." By the constant fall of waterdrops, a pitcher is filled; likewise the unwise person, accumulating evil little by little, becomes full of evil.

Do not think lightly of merit, saying, "It will not come to me." By the constant fall of waterdrops, a pitcher is filled; likewise the wise person, accumulating merit little by little, becomes full of merit.

DHAMMAPADA 121–122

249.

The king said: 'Is ordination a good thing?'

'Yes, a good thing and a beautiful [thing].'

'But did the Buddha obtain it, or not?'

'Great king, when the Blessed One attained omniscience at the foot of the tree of Knowledge, that was to him an ordination. There was no conferring of ordination upon him at the hands of others—[not] in the way that the Blessed One laid down regulations for his disciples, never to be transgressed by them their lives long!'

'Very true, Nāgasena!'

MILINDAPAÑHA 76

250.

He who knows that all things are his mind,
That all with which he meets are friendly,
Is ever joyful.

HUNDRED THOUSAND SONGS OF MILAREPA

251.

If in the end the law of entire destruction (is exacted) what use is there in indolence and pride? Covetous desire (lust) is the greatest (source of) sorrow, appearing as a friend, in secret 'tis our enemy.

FO-SHO-HING-TSAN-KING 1813

252.

There is, O monks, a realm, where there is neither earth, nor water, nor fire, nor wind, neither the sphere of boundless consciousness, nor the sphere of nothingness, nor the sphere of neither-perception-nor-nonperception, neither this world nor the next world, nor both together, nor moon and sun. This, O monks, I call neither a going, nor a coming, nor a standing, nor dying, nor being born. It is without a foothold, without a beginning, without a foundation. This indeed is the end of suffering.

UDĀNA 8.1

253.

I like to walk alone on country paths, rice plants and wild grasses on both sides, putting each foot down on the earth in mindfulness, knowing that I walk on the wondrous earth. In such moments, existence is a miraculous and mysterious reality. People usually consider walking on water or in thin air a miracle. But I think the real miracle is not to walk either on water or in thin air, but to walk on earth. Every day we are engaged in a miracle which we don't even recognize: a blue sky, white clouds, green leaves, the black, curious eyes of a child—our own two eyes. All is a miracle.

THICH NHAT HANH; *MIRACLE OF MINDFULNESS*

254.

When Ts'ao-shan left Tung-shan, Tung-shan asked him, "Where
   are you going?"

Ts'ao-shan said, "To an unchanging place."

Tung-shan retorted, "If it is an unchanging place, how can there
   be any going?"

Ts'ao-shan replied, "The going is also unchanging."

TUNG-SHAN; *FIVE HOUSES OF ZEN*

255.

At Sāvatthi, we are told, on a certain great Fast-day, five hundred women took upon themselves the obligations of Fast-day and went to the monastery. Visākhā approached the oldest women of the company and asked, "Women, for what purpose have you assumed the obligations of Fast-day?" They replied, "Because we seek a heavenly reward." When she put the question to the women who had reached middle life, they replied, "To obtain release from the power of our husbands." When she asked the young women, they replied, "That we may conceive a child as soon as possible." Finally she asked the maidens, who replied, "That we may obtain husbands while we are still young."

When Visākhā had heard the replies of all, she then went to the Teacher, taking the women with her, and told him each of the replies in order. The Teacher listened to the replies and then said, "Visākhā, in the case of living beings here in the world, birth, old age, sickness, and death are like cowherds with staves in their hands. Birth sends them to old age, and old age to sickness, and sickness to death; they cut life short as though they cut with an axe. But despite this, there are none that desire absence of rebirth; rebirth is all they desire."

DHAMMAPADA COMMENTARY TO VERSE 135

256.

The pain of birth, old age, disease, and death press heavily upon the world, but adding "passion" to the score, what is this but to increase our foes when pressed by foes?

But rather, seeing how the world is pressed by throngs of grief, we ought to encourage in us love (a loving heart), and as the world (all flesh) produces grief on grief, so should we add as antidotes unnumbered remedies.

FO-SHO-HING-TSAN-KING 1827–1828

257.

If a man string putrid fish
On a blade of *kusa* grass,
That same grass will putrid smell.
So with him who follows fools.

If a man wrap frankincense
In a leaf, that leaf smells sweet.
So with those who follow sages.

ITIVUTTAKA 76

258.

If, as the disciple fares along, he meets no companion who is better or equal, let him firmly pursue his solitary career. There is no fellowship with the foolish.

DHAMMAPADA 61

259.

When we say, "I take refuge in the Buddha," we should also understand that "The Buddha takes refuge in me," because without the second part the first part is not complete. The Buddha needs us for awakening, understanding, and love to be real things and not just concepts. They must be real things that have real effects on life. Whenever I say, "I take refuge in the Buddha," I hear "Buddha takes refuge in me."

THICH NHAT HANH; *BEING PEACE*

260.

If you can only rid yourselves of conceptual thought, you will have accomplished everything.

HUANG PO; *ZEN TEACHING OF HUANG PO*

261.

The source of all good, evil, weal and harm lies with actions, speech and thoughts. Did you bring your actions, speech and thoughts with you today? Or have you left them at home? This is where you must look, right here. You don't have to look very far away. Look at your actions, speech and thoughts.

AJAHN CHAH; *LIVING DHAMMA*

262.

The unwise man, lacking understanding,
Behaves as if he were his own worst enemy,
Committing evil deeds
That produce bitter fruit.

DHAMMAPADA 66

263.

Compassion is characterized as promoting the aspect of allaying suffering. Its function resides in not [enduring] others' suffering. It is manifested as non-cruelty. Its proximate cause is to see helplessness in those overwhelmed by suffering. It succeeds when it makes cruelty subside, and it fails when it produces sorrow.

BUDDHAGHOSA; *VISUDDHIMAGGA 318*

264.

They are happy indeed who own nothing at all;
Those with highest knowledge own nothing at all.
See how people who own things are afflicted,
Bound to others by their obligations.

UDĀNA 2.6

265.

Whatever is transitory indeed has a false nature.

(But) nibbāna does not have a false nature. That the noble ones know truly. Because of the full comprehension of the truth they indeed are without craving, quenched.

SUTTA NIPĀTA 757–758

266.

Let none find fault with others; let none see the omissions and commissions of others. But let one see one's own acts, done and undone.

DHAMMAPADA 50

267.

[W]e also discussed the relative virtues of the arhat and the bodhisattva. [Ahjahn Chah] ended our discussion by saying, "Don't be
an arhat. Don't be a Buddha. Don't be anything at all. Being something makes problems. So don't be anything. You don't have to be
something, he doesn't have to be something, I don't have to be
something. . . ." He paused, and then said, "Sometimes when I
think about it, I don't want to say anything."

PAUL BREITER; *VENERABLE FATHER*

268.

Self-awareness, self-illumination, self-liberation, these three,
When arising, arise from the mind itself.
When disappearing, they disappear into the mind itself.

The unborn, unceasing, and unexpressed, these three,
When emerging, arise from the nature of being itself.
When disappearing, they disappear into the nature of being
itself.

HUNDRED THOUSAND SONGS: SELECTIONS FROM MILAREPA,
POET-SAINT OF TIBET

269.

The mind is something more radiant than anything else can be, but because counterfeits—passing defilements—come and obscure it, it loses its radiance, like the sun when obscured by clouds. Don't go thinking that the sun goes after the clouds. Instead, the clouds come drifting along and obscure the sun.

AJAAN MUN; *HEART RELEASED*

270.

Even as rain breaks through an ill-thatched house,
So lust breaks through an ill-trained mind.

Even as rain breaks not through a well-thatched house,
So lust breaks not through a well-trained mind.

DHAMMAPADA 13–14

271.

Of the divine state of love the near enemy is lust, because, like love, it sees good qualities. It is like a foe lurking near a man. Quickly it finds access. Hence love should be well protected from lust. Ill-will is the distant enemy. From its dissimilarity in nature it is like a man's foe dwelling in a mountain fastness, and so on. Hence love should be developed secure from ill-will. It is impossible that one should develop love and at the same time get angry.

BUDDHAGHOSA; *VISUDDHIMAGGA 318–319*

272.

The king said: 'Nāgasena, is there any one who after death is not reindividualized [reborn]?'

'Some are so, and some not.'

'Who are they?'

'A sinful being is reindividualized, a sinless one is not.'

'Will you be reindividualized?'

'If when I die, I die with craving for existence in my heart, yes; but if not, no.'

'Very good, Nāgasena!'

MILINDAPAÑHA 32

273.

Negligence produces a lot of dirt. As in a house, so in the mind, only a very little dirt collects in a day or two, but if it goes on for many years, it will grow into a vast heap of refuse.

SUTTA NIPĀTA; COMMENTARY TO VERSE 334

274.

Once the sense of self is transcended, its polar opposite—the sense of something standing in contradistinction to a self—is transcended as well. . . . For a person who has attained the goal, experience occurs with no 'subject' or 'object' superimposed on it, no construing of experience or thing experienced. There is simply the experience in & of itself.

ṬHĀNISSARO BHIKKHU; *MIND LIKE FIRE UNBOUND*

275.

Because it lacks consciousness, I must admit that a word cannot praise me. Undoubtedly, the cause of my delight is that another is delighted with me.

But what does it matter to me whether another's delight is in me or someone else? His alone is the pleasure of that delight. Not even a trifling part of it is mine.

ŚĀNTIDEVA; *BODHICARYĀVATĀRA 6.94–6.95*

276.

Nowhere!
Not in the sky,
Nor in the midst of the sea,
Nor deep in the mountains,
Can you hide from your own mischief.

Not in the sky,
Nor in the midst of the ocean,
Nor deep in the mountains,
Nowhere
Can you hide from your own death.

DHAMMAPADA 127–128

277.

In the beginner's mind there are many possibilities; in the expert's mind there are few.

SHUNRYU SUZUKI; *ZEN MIND, BEGINNER'S MIND*

278.

You have always been one with the Buddha, so do not pretend you can ATTAIN to this oneness by various practices.

HUANG PO; *ZEN TEACHING OF HUANG PO*

279.

Is true contemplating the same as thinking?

We use thinking as a tool, but the knowing that arises because of its use is above and beyond the process of thinking; it leads to our not being fooled by our thinking any more. You recognize that all thinking is merely the movement of the mind, and also that the knowing is not born and doesn't die. What do you think all this movement called 'mind' comes out of? What we talk about as the mind—all the activity—is just the conventional mind. It's not the real mind at all. What is real just IS, it's not arising and it's not passing away.

AJAHN CHAH; *SEEING THE WAY*

280.

It is essential that you neither despise nor grasp for either the realm of activity or that of quietude, and that you continue your practice assiduously.

Frequently you may feel that you are getting nowhere with practice in the midst of activity, whereas the quietistic approach brings unexpected results. Yet rest assured that those who use the quietistic approach can never hope to enter into meditation in the midst of activity.

HAKUIN; *ZEN MASTER HAKUIN*

281.

Due to having many parts there is no unity,
There is not anything without parts.
Further, without one, there is not many.
Also, without existence there is no non-existence.

NĀGĀRJUNA; *PRECIOUS GARLAND 71*

282.

Turn away from mischief.
Again and again, turn away,
Before sorrow befalls you.

Set your heart on doing good.
Do it over and over again,
And you will be filled with joy.

DHAMMAPADA 117–118

283.

The charity which unstores wealth leads to returns of well-stored fruit. Giving away our food we get more strength, giving away our clothes we get more beauty. . . .

FO-SHO-HING-TSAN-KING 1516

284.

There is, monks, this one way to the purification of beings, for the overcoming of sorrow and distress, for the disappearance of pain and sadness, for the gaining of the right path, for the realization of Nibbāna: that is to say the four foundations of mindfulness.

What are the four? Here, monks, a monk abides contemplating body as body, ardent, clearly aware and mindful, having put aside hankering and fretting for the world; he abides contemplating feelings as feelings . . . ; he abides contemplating mind as mind . . . ; he abides contemplating mind-objects as mind-objects, ardent, clearly aware and mindful, having put aside hankering and fretting for the world.

DĪGHA NIKĀYA ii 290

285.

Listen to the sound of water. Listen to the water running through chasms and rocks. It is the minor streams that make a loud noise; the great waters flow silently.

The hollow resounds and the full is still. Foolishness is like a half-filled pot; the wise man is a lake full of water.

SUTTA NIPĀTA 720–721

286.

Monks, there are these three elements of escape. What three?

This escape from lusts which is renunciation; this escape from forms which is the formless existence; and this escape from whatsoever has become, is compounded, has arisen by the law of causation, which is making to cease. These are the three elements of escape.

ITIVUTTAKA 72

287.

He becomes one who acts in full awareness when going forward
and returning; who acts in full awareness when looking ahead
and looking away; who acts in full awareness when flexing and
extending his limbs; who acts in full awareness when wearing his
robes and carrying his outer robe and bowl; who acts in full awareness when eating, drinking, consuming food, and tasting; who acts
in full awareness when defecating and urinating; who acts in full
awareness when walking, standing, sitting, falling asleep, waking
up, talking, and keeping silent.

MAJJHIMA-NIKĀYA i.181

288.

The mind is often compared to a horseman and the breath to the horse. A wild and untamed horse is difficult for the rider; a very good and well-trained horse is quite useful. If both rider and horse are extremely well trained and skilled, an excellent combination has been made.

CHÖKYI NYIMA RINPOCHE; *UNION OF MAHAMUDRA AND DZOGCHEN*

289.

Just understand that birth-and-death is itself nirvāṇa. There is nothing such as birth and death to be avoided; there is nothing such as nirvāṇa to be sought. Only when you realize this are you free from birth and death.

DŌGEN; *MOON IN A DEWDROP*

290.

The image of an extinguished fire carried no connotations of annihilation for the early Buddhists. Rather, the aspects of fire that to them had significance for the mind-fire analogy are these: Fire, when burning, is in a state of agitation, dependence, attachment, & entrapment—both clinging & being stuck to its sustenance. Extinguished, it becomes calm, independent, indeterminate, & unattached: It lets go of its sustenance and is released.

ṬHĀNISSARO BHIKKHU; *MIND LIKE FIRE UNBOUND*

291.

"What do you think about this, sire? When the flame of a great burning mass of fire has gone out, is it possible to point to that flame and say that it is either here or there?"

"O no, revered sir, that flame has stopped, it has disappeared."

"Even so, sire, the Lord has attained final nibbāna in the element of nibbāna that has no substrate remaining (for future birth); it is not possible to point to the Lord who has gone home and say that he is either here or there; but, sire, it is possible to point to the Lord by means of the body of Dhamma, for Dhamma, sire, was taught by the Lord."

MILINDAPAÑHA 73

292.

Many people are afraid to empty their minds lest they may plunge into the Void. They do not know that their own Mind is the Void. The ignorant eschew phenomena but not thought; the wise eschew thought but not phenomena.

HUANG PO; *ZEN TEACHING OF HUANG PO*

293.

A "virtuous friend" though he be gentle is not to be compared with right reflection (thought)—right thought kept well in the mind, no evil thing can ever enter there.

FO-SHO-HING-TSAN-KING 2070

294.

Do you not see—the clouds on the highest mountain gather and disperse of themselves; what "far" or "near" is there? The flowing water at the bottom of the canyon follows the curves and the straits, without "this" or "that."

The everyday life of people is like clouds and water, but clouds and water are free while people are not. If they would get to be as free as clouds and water, where would people's compulsive mundane routines arise?

DŌGEN; *RATIONAL ZEN*

295.

A sage does not speak in terms of being equal, lower or higher.
Calmed and without selfishness he neither grasps nor rejects.

SUTTA NIPĀTA 954

296.

Even if you seek to harm an enemy,
You should remove your own defects and cultivate good qualities.
Through that you will help yourself,
And the enemy will be displeased.

NĀGĀRJUNA; *PRECIOUS GARLAND 132*

297.

Those who have great realization about delusion are buddhas. Those who are greatly deluded within realization are sentient beings.

DŌGEN; *FLOWERS FALL (SHŌBŌGENZŌ GENJŌKŌAN)*

298.

The value of Dhamma isn't to be found in books. Those are just the external appearances of Dhamma, they're not the realization of Dhamma as a personal experience. **If you realize the Dhamma you realize your own mind,** you see the truth there. When the truth becomes apparent it cuts off the stream of delusion.

AJAHN CHAH; *LIVING DHAMMA*

299.

Bhikkhus, all is burning. And what is the all that is burning?

The eye is burning, forms are burning, eye-consciousness is burning, eye-contact is burning, also whatever is felt as pleasant or painful or neither-painful-nor-pleasant that arises with eye-contact for its indispensable condition, that too is burning. . . .

The ear is burning, sounds are burning . . .
The nose is burning, odors are burning . . .
The tongue is burning, flavors are burning . . .
The body is burning, tangibles are burning . . .

The mind is burning, ideas are burning. . . . Burning with what? Burning with the fire of lust, with the fire of hate, with the fire of delusion. I say it is burning with birth, aging and death, with sorrows, with lamentations, with pains, with griefs, with despairs.

SAṂYUTTA NIKĀYA XXXV. 1, 28

300.

His the knife, and mine the body—the twofold cause of suffering.
He has grasped the knife, I my body. At which is there anger?

ŚĀNTIDEVA; *BODHICARYĀVATĀRA 6.43*

301.

He who has put away evil, who is humble, free
    from impurity, self restrained, versed in knowledge,
    leading a holy life,
That man may be truly called a Brāhmaṇa.
For him there are no desires anywhere in the world.

UDĀNA 1.4

302.

The purpose of studying Buddhism is not to study Buddhism, but to study ourselves.

SHUNRYU SUZUKI; *ZEN MIND, BEGINNER'S MIND*

303.

It is crucial for you to understand what meditation is. It is not some special posture, and it's not just a set of mental exercises. Meditation is the cultivation of mindfulness and the application of that mindfulness once cultivated. You do not have to sit to meditate. You can meditate while washing the dishes. You can meditate in the shower, or roller skating, or typing letters. Meditation is awareness, and it must be applied to each and every activity of one's life. This isn't easy.

HENEPOLA GUNARATANA; *MINDFULNESS IN PLAIN ENGLISH*

304.

The mind and feeling are just like oil and water; they are in the same bottle but they don't mix. Even if we are sick or in pain, we still know the feeling as feeling, the mind as mind. We know the painful or comfortable states but we don't identify with them. We stay only with peace: the peace beyond both comfort and pain.

AJAHN CHAH; *TASTE OF FREEDOM*

305.

"Look how he abused me and beat me,
How he threw me down and robbed me."
Live with such thoughts and you live in hate.

"Look how he abused me and beat me,
How he threw me down and robbed me."
Abandon such thoughts, and live in love.

In this world
Hate never yet dispelled hate.
Only love dispels hate.
This is the law,
Ancient and inexhaustible.

DHAMMAPADA 3–5

306.

In *becoming an enlightened being*, this does not destroy the *living being*, or take it away, or lose it; nevertheless, it does mean having shed it.

DŌGEN; *RATIONAL ZEN*

307.

Without relation to 'good' there is no 'bad', in dependence on which we form the idea of 'good'. Therefore 'good' is unintelligible.

There is no 'good' unrelated to 'bad'; yet we form our idea of 'bad' in dependence on it. There is, therefore, no 'bad'.

As 'good' is non-existent how can there be desire? As 'bad' is non-existent how can there be aversion?

NĀGĀRJUNA; *MŪLAMADHYAMAKA-KĀRIKĀ XXIII, 10–12*

308.

The bliss of lusts and heaven-world equal not
One sixteenth of the bliss of craving's ending.

UDĀNA 2.2

309.

Where there is great hatred, are the fetters of hell.
Where there is great avarice, are the fetters of the tortured spirits.
Where there is great ignorance, are the fetters of the beasts.
Where there is great lust, are the fetters of man.
Where there is great envy, are the fetters of the demigods.
Where there is great pride, are the fetters of the gods.
These are the six fetters of non-liberation.

HUNDRED THOUSAND SONGS: SELECTIONS FROM MILAREPA,
POET-SAINT OF TIBET

310.

Erroneous views keep us in defilement
While right views remove us from it,
But when we are in a position to discard both of them
We are then absolutely pure.

THE SUTRA OF HUI NENG

311.

What is the Sound of the Single Hand? When you clap together both hands a sharp sound is heard; when you raise the one hand there is neither sound nor smell.

HAKUIN; *ZEN MASTER HAKUIN*

312.

If men but knew their own nature, they would not dwell (indulge) in sorrow; everything that lives, whate'er it be, all this is subject to destruction's law;

I have already told you plainly, the law (nature) of things "joined" is to "separate"; the principle of kindness and of love is not abiding, 'tis better then to reject this pitiful and doting heart.

All things around us bear the stamp of instant change; born, they perish; no self-sufficiency; those who would wish to keep them long, find in the end no room for doing so.

FO-SHO-HING-TSAN-KING 1860–1862

313.

What is laughter, what is joy, when the world is ever burning?
Shrouded by darkness, would you not seek the light?

DHAMMAPADA 146

314.

Develop the mind of equilibrium. You will always be getting praise and blame, but do not let either affect the poise of the mind: follow the calmness, the absence of pride.

SUTTA NIPĀTA 702

315.

In extinguishing the three realms, arahants don't fly up into the realms of sensuality, form and formlessness. They stay right where they are. The same was true of the Buddha: When he extinguished the three realms, he was sitting in one spot, under the Bodhi tree. He didn't fly up into the three realms. He extinguished them at the mind—for right there in the mind is where the three realms exist.

Those who aim at extinguishing the three realms should thus extinguish them in their own hearts. Only then will they obliterate activity—the act of supposing—from the heart, leaving just activityless-ness. This is the primal heart, the primal Dhamma, which knows no death.

AJAAN MUN; *HEART RELEASED*

316.

Dig the pond, don't wait for the moonlight; when the pond is complete, the moonlight will naturally be there.

HUNG-CHIH; *FIVE HOUSES OF ZEN*

317.

We should always live in the dark empty sky. The sky is always the sky. Even though clouds and lightning come, the sky is not disturbed. Even if the flashing of enlightenment comes, our practice forgets all about it. Then it is ready for another enlightenment.

SHUNRYU SUZUKI; *ZEN MIND, BEGINNER'S MIND*

318.

Where neither water nor yet earth
Nor fire nor air gain a foothold,
There gleam no stars, no sun sheds light,
There shines no moon, yet there no darkness reigns.
When a sage, a brahmin, has come to know this
For himself through his own experience,
Then he is freed from form and formlessness,
Freed from pleasure and from pain.

UDĀNA 1.10

319.

Due to having faith one relies on the practices,
Due to having wisdom one truly knows.
Of these two wisdom is the chief,
Faith is its prerequisite.

NĀGĀRJUNA; *PRECIOUS GARLAND* 5

320.

Trivial thoughts, insignificant thoughts,
When followed they distract the mind.
Not understanding those thoughts
The roaming mind runs back and forth.
But by understanding those thoughts
One ardent and mindful restrains the mind.
An awakened one has overcome them completely
So they do not arise to distract the mind.

UDĀNA 4.1

321.

For one who is in the habit of constantly honoring and respecting the elders, four blessings increase—age, beauty, bliss, and strength.

DHAMMAPADA 109

322.

Monks, in giving a meal, a giver gives five things to an almsman. What five?

He gives life, beauty, ease, strength and wit; but in giving these he becomes a partaker in each quality, in heaven and among men.

ANGUTTARA-NIKĀYA iii.42

323.

Walking the spiritual path properly is a very subtle process; it is not something to jump into naively. There are numerous sidetracks which lead to a distorted, ego-centered version of spirituality; we can deceive ourselves into thinking we are developing spiritually when instead we are strengthening our egocentricity through spiritual techniques. This fundamental distortion may be referred to as *spiritual materialism*.

CHÖGYAM TRUNGPA; *CUTTING THROUGH SPIRITUAL MATERIALISM*

324.

Just as, O Bhikkhus, the Great Ocean has but one taste, the taste of salt, even so, O Bhikkhus, this doctrine has but one taste, the taste of Deliverance.

UDĀNA 5.5

325.

Mindfulness is the path to immortality.
Negligence is the path to death.
The vigilant never die,
Whereas the negligent are the living dead.

With this understanding,
The wise, having developed a high degree of mindfulness,
Rejoice in mindfulness,
Paying heed to each step on the path.

These awakened ones,
Dedicated to meditation,
Striving actively and vigorously,
Attain nirvāṇa, the ultimate security.

DHAMMAPADA 21–23

326.

It is easy for the good person to do good deeds,
but for the evil one it is difficult to do good deeds.
It is easy for the evil person to do bad deeds,
but it is difficult for the good one to do bad deeds.

UDĀNA 5.8

327.

How to cope with wavering thoughts?
Versatile are flying clouds,
Yet from the sky they're not apart.
Mighty are the ocean's waves,
Yet they are not separate from the sea.
Heavy and thick are banks of fog,
Yet from the air they're not apart.
Frantic runs the mind in voidness,
Yet from the Void it never separates.

HUNDRED THOUSAND SONGS OF MILAREPA

328.

There is pleasure when a sore is scratched,
But to be without sores is more pleasurable still.
Just so, there are pleasures in worldly desires,
But to be without desires is more pleasurable still.

NĀGĀRJUNA; *PRECIOUS GARLAND 169*

329.

As the fish, taken out of its watery home and thrown on land, thrashes around, so does the mind tremble, while freeing itself from the dominion of Māra (the Evil One).

DHAMMAPADA 34

330.

Mind cannot see itself—
Subject and object *cannot* be dual;
Therefore, to see the mind
You must look and probe with the eye of wisdom.

When probed and examined analytically
With such analytic investigation
The mind is like the wick of a lamp
Illumined only through its own radiance.

*DRINKING THE MOUNTAIN STREAM: SONGS OF
TIBET'S BELOVED SAINT, MILAREPA*

331.

Experiencing emptiness is also experiencing peace, and the potential of peace is its unfolding as harmony among all people, animals, plants, and things. The precepts formulate this harmony, showing how the absence of killing and stealing is the very condition of mercy and charity.

ROBERT AITKEN; *MIND OF CLOVER*

332.

Anything which is created must, sooner or later, die. If enlightenment were created in such a way, there would always be the possibility of ego reasserting itself, causing a return to the confused state. Enlightenment is permanent because we have not produced it; we have merely discovered it. In the Buddhist tradition the analogy of the sun appearing from behind the clouds is often used to explain the discovery of enlightenment. In meditation practice we clear away the confusion of ego in order to glimpse the awakened state. The absence of ignorance, of being crowded in, of paranoia, opens up a tremendous view of life. One discovers a different way of being.

CHÖGYAM TRUNGPA; *CUTTING THROUGH*
SPIRITUAL MATERIALISM

333.

'There is no spot, O king, where Nirvāṇa is situate, and yet Nirvāṇa is, and he who orders his life right will, by careful attention,
realize Nirvāṇa. Just as fire exists, and yet there is no place where
fire (by itself) is stored up. But if a man rubs two sticks together
the fire comes; just so, O king, Nirvāṇa exists, though there is no
spot where it is stored up. And he who orders his life aright will,
by careful attention, realize Nirvāṇa.'

MILINDAPAÑHA 327

334.

Without hope of reward
Provide help to others.
Bear suffering alone,
And share your pleasures with beggars.

NĀGĀRJUNA; *PRECIOUS GARLAND 272*

335.

There is, bhikkhus, a not-born, a not-brought-to-being, a not-made, a not-formed. If, bhikkhus, there were not that not-born, not-brought-to-being, not-made, not-formed, no escape would be discerned from what is born, brought-to-being, made, formed. But since there is a not-born, a not-brought-to-being, a not-made, a not-formed, therefore there is discerned an escape from what is born, brought-to-being, made, formed.

ITIVUTTAKA 43

336.

All beings tremble before violence.
All fear death.
All love life.

See yourself in others.
Then whom can you hurt?
What harm can you do?

DHAMMAPADA 129–130

337.

Things in themselves are void,
So never cling to Voidness
Lest you stray [into] formalism.

HUNDRED THOUSAND SONGS OF MILAREPA

338.

The impulse "I want" and the impulse "I'll have"—lose them!
That is where most people get stuck—without those, you can use
your eyes to guide you through this suffering state.

SUTTA NIPĀTA 706

There was once a woman who was arrogant and proud. She decided she wanted to attain enlightenment, so she asked all the authorities how to do that. One said, "Well, if you climb to the top of this very high mountain, you'll find a cave there. Sitting inside that cave is a very wise old woman, and she will tell you." So the woman thought, "Good, I'll do that. Nothing but the best." Having endured great hardships, she finally found this cave, and sure enough, sitting there was this very gentle, spiritual-looking old woman in white clothes who smiled at her beatifically. Overcome with awe and respect, she prostrated at the feet of this woman and said, "I want to attain enlightenment. Show me how." The wise woman looked at her with her beatific smile and asked, "Are you sure you want to attain enlightenment?" And the woman said, "Of course I'm sure." Whereupon the smiling woman turned into a demon, stood up brandishing a great big stick, and started chasing her, saying, "Now! Now! Now!" For the rest of her life, that lady could never get away from the demon who was always saying, "Now!"

PEMA CHÖDRÖN; *WISDOM OF NO ESCAPE*

340.

The Dharma Path is to keep walking forward. But the true Dharma has no going forward, no going backward, and no standing still.

AJAHN CHAH; *STILL FOREST POOL*

341.

Conquer your foe by force, you increase his enmity; conquer by love, and you will reap no after-sorrow.

FO-SHO-HING-TSAN-KING 2241

The king said: 'He who will not be reborn [one who is enlightened], Nāgasena, does he still feel any painful sensation?'

The Elder replied: 'Some he feels and some not.'

'Which are they?'

'He may feel bodily pain, O king; but mental pain he would not.'

'How would that be so?'

'Because the causes, proximate or remote, of bodily pain still continue, he would be liable to it. But the causes, proximate or remote, of mental agony having ceased, he could not feel it. For it has been said by the Blessed One: "One kind of pain he suffers, bodily pain: but not mental."'

'Then why, Sir, does he not die?'

'The Arahant, O king, has need neither to curry favor nor to bear malice. He shakes not down the unripe fruit, but awaits the full time of its maturity. For it has been said, O king, by the Elder, Sāriputta, the Commander of the faith:

"It is not death, it is not life I welcome;
As the hireling his wage, so do I bide my time.
It is not death, it is not life I want;
Mindful and thoughtful do I bide my time."'

'Well put, Nāgasena!'

343.

Opening the door on voidness of identity,
Clear awareness floods everywhere,
And though everywhere, nowhere is an identity found.

DRINKING THE MOUNTAIN STREAM: SONGS OF
TIBET'S BELOVED SAINT, MILAREPA

344.

"I am not, I will not be.
I have not, I will not have."
That frightens all the childish
And extinguishes fear in the wise.

NĀGĀRJUNA; *PRECIOUS GARLAND 26*

345.

Abandoning malicious speech, he abstains from malicious speech; he does not repeat elsewhere what he has heard here in order to divide (those people) from these, nor does he repeat to these people what he has heard elsewhere in order to divide (these people) from those; thus he is one who reunites those who are divided, a promoter of friendships, who enjoys concord, rejoices in concord, delights in concord, a speaker of words that promote concord.

MAJJHIMA-NIKĀYA i.179

346.

The fundamental Doctrine of the Dharma is that there are no Dharmas, yet that this Doctrine of No-Dharma is in itself a Dharma; and now that the No-Dharma Doctrine has been transmitted, how can the Doctrine of the Dharma be a Dharma?

HUANG PO; *ZEN TEACHING OF HUANG PO*

347.

A view is true or false only when one is judging how accurately it refers to something else. If one is regarding it simply as an event in & of itself, true & false no longer apply. Thus for the Tathāgata— who no longer needs to impose notions of subject or object on experience, and can regard sights, sounds, feelings, & thoughts purely in & of themselves—views are not necessarily true or false, but can simply serve as phenomena to be experienced. . . . As a result, the mind can see conditioned events in their suchness—'such are the aggregates, such their origin, such their disappearance'—and is left free to its own Suchness: unrestrained, uninfluenced by anything of any sort.

ṬHĀNISSARO BHIKKHU; *MIND LIKE FIRE UNBOUND*

348.

If you think you see both
Destruction and becoming,
Then you see destruction and becoming
Through impaired vision.

NĀGĀRJUNA; *MŪLAMADHYAMAKA-KĀRIKĀ XXI, 11*

349.

Should we free our mind from attachment to all 'things,' the Path becomes clear; otherwise, we put ourselves under restraint.

THE SUTRA OF HUI NENG

And the king said: 'What is the object, Sir, of your renunciation, and what [is] the summum bonum at which you aim?'

'Why do you ask? Our renunciation is to the end that this sorrow may perish away, and that no further sorrow may arise; the complete passing away, without cleaving to the world, is our highest aim.'

'How now, Sir! Is it for such high reasons that all members of it have joined the Order?'

'Certainly not, Sire. Some for those reasons, but some have left the world in terror at the tyranny of kings. Some have joined us to be safe from being robbed, some harassed by debt, and some perhaps to gain a livelihood.'

'But for what object, Sir, did you yourself join?'

'I was received into the Order when I was a mere boy; I knew not then the ultimate aim. But I thought: "They are wise scholars, these Buddhist Samaṇas, they will be able to teach me." And by them I have been taught; and now do I both know and understand what is at once the reason for, and the advantage of renunciation.'

'Well put, Nāgasena!'

MILINDAPAÑHA 31–32

351.

Although there are countless teachings that instruct how to obtain enlightenment in a future life, almost all of them are nothing more than expedients. As the ultimate instruction there is simply no teaching that is superior to the true practice of the awakening to one's own nature.

HAKUIN; *ZEN MASTER HAKUIN*

352.

There are those with *enlightened knowledge*: this is not knowledge by birth, or knowledge by learning: it is beginningless in *here*, having transcended the bounds of self and other, it is *being unbound* by *knowledge of self and other*.

DŌGEN; *RATIONAL ZEN*

353.

"I, without grasping, will pass beyond sorrow,
And I will attain nirvāṇa," one says.
Whoever grasps like this
Has great grasping.

NĀGĀRJUNA; *MŪLAMADHYAMAKA-KĀRIKĀ XVI, 9*

354.

To probe deep into your roots:
The ignorance and confusion are you yourself.
The preconceptions which are yourself
Are envoys and agents sent by yourself.

DRINKING THE MOUNTAIN STREAM: SONGS OF
TIBET'S BELOVED SAINT, MILAREPA

355.

The mind is not just 'oneness' or a singular entity because it manifests in manifold ways. It is not a plurality or many things, either, because these numerous manifestations all have one essence. No one can describe its nature saying, "It is exactly like this!" It is indescribable, unutterable, inconceivable, nonarising, unceasing, and nondwelling, like the essence of space. Mind nature is discovered within the experience of awareness and is cognized individually.

CHÖKYI NYIMA RINPOCHE; *UNION OF
MAHAMUDRA AND DZOGCHEN*

356.

Simply keep putting everything down, and know that that is what you are doing. You don't need to be always checking up on yourself, worrying about things like 'How much samādhi'—it will always be the right amount. Whatever arises in your practice, let it go; know it all as uncertain, impermanent. Remember that! It's all uncertain. Be finished with all of it. This is the Way that will take you to the source—to your Original Mind.

AJAHN CHAH; *SEEING THE WAY*

357.

This is an old saying, O Atula, not one merely of today: "They blame him who remains silent, they blame him who speaks much, they even blame him who speaks in moderation." There is none in this world who is not blamed.

There never existed, nor will there ever exist, nor does there exist today anyone who is always scorned or always praised.

DHAMMAPADA 227–228

358.

You should know that so far as Buddha-nature is concerned, there is no difference between an enlightened man and an ignorant one. What makes the difference is that one realizes it, while the other is ignorant of it.

THE SUTRA OF HUI NENG

359.

"But it is the flesh that I enjoy."
If this is what I wish to touch and behold,
Why do I not desire it in its natural state
Devoid of any mind?

Furthermore, any mind that I may desire
Is unable to be touched or beheld,
And whatever I am able to touch will not be mental;
So why indulge in this meaningless copulation?

ŚĀNTIDEVA; *BODHICARYĀVATĀRA 8.54–8.55*

360.

To disregard oneself, this is the best dharma.
This is the best service to Buddha's religion.
Practicing meditation for life is the best gift
To those sentient beings without protection.

HUNDRED THOUSAND SONGS: SELECTIONS FROM MILAREPA,
POET-SAINT OF TIBET

361.

Clearly, buddha-dharma is not practiced for one's own sake, and even less for the sake of fame and profit. Just for the sake of buddha-dharma you should practice it.

All buddhas' compassion and sympathy for sentient beings are neither for their own sake nor for others. It is just the nature of buddha-dharma.

DŌGEN; *MOON IN A DEWDROP*

362.

Herein, Meghiya, a monk has a good friend, a good companion, a good comrade. For the emancipation of the mind of the unripe, this is the first condition conducive to the ripening.

ANGUTTARA-NIKĀYA iv.356

363.

Treat your anger with the utmost respect and tenderness, for it is no other than yourself. Do not suppress it—simply be aware of it. Awareness is like the sun. When it shines on things, they are transformed. When you are aware that you are angry, your anger is transformed. If you destroy anger, you destroy the Buddha, for Buddha and Māra are of the same essence. Mindfully dealing with anger is like taking the hand of a little brother.

THICH NHAT HANH; QUOTED IN *MIND OF CLOVER*

364.

When you behold the void nature of Mind,
Analyze it not as one or many
Lest you fall into the void-of-annihilation!
Son, rest yourself without wandering thoughts.

HUNDRED THOUSAND SONGS OF MILAREPA

365.

In Seattle someone had asked [Ahjahn Chah] to describe how he prepared his mind for meditation, and he said, "I just keep it where it always is."

PAUL BREITER; *VENERABLE FATHER*

GLOSSARY

Words defined elsewhere in the glossary are printed in boldface the first time they appear in a given definition. Languages are indicated in italics and in parentheses after each word, and after each alternate spelling for languages actually quoted.

Chi—Chinese   *Skt*—Sanskrit
Eng—English   *Thai*—Thai
Jpn—Japanese   *Tib*—Tibetan
Pali—Pali

Word or Name	Definition
Ahjahn Chah, Ajahn Chah *(Thai)*	(1918–1992) Thai monk and meditation teacher, around whom the monastery **Wat Pah Pong** and more than 150 branch monasteries have formed across Thailand and around the world. Known for teaching a strict traditional forest practice.
Amitābha *(Skt)*	In **Mahāyāna Buddhism,** the **Buddha** of infinite light, who, as the embodiment of perfect compassion, has created a beautiful, blissful **Pure Land,** where he assists believers in attaining enlightenment.

Ānanda *(Pali, Skt)*	The **Buddha's** personal attendant for twenty-five years and one of the Buddha's principal disciples. He was a first cousin of the Buddha, and it was Ānanda who, at the first **Buddhist** council after the death of the Buddha, recited the whole of the Buddha's teachings from memory. They are Ānanda's words that begin every Buddhist sutra, "Thus have I heard . . ."
Arahant *(Pali)*, Arhat *(Skt)*	Literally, worthy one. One who has eliminated all mental defilements through seeing personally the three characteristics of existence; that all compounded things are impermanent, that all compounded things are unsatisfactory, and that all things are without self. The highest goal for **Theravāda Buddhism,** as opposed to the **bodhisattva** ideal in **Mahāyāna** Buddhism.
Aranyabho *(Pali)*	A young English novice monk at **Wat Pah Pong** monastery.
Atula *(Pali)*	A lay disciple who complained to the **Buddha** about the length of the sermons he received from various **Buddhist** monks whom he approached for teachings.
Bāhiya *(Pali)*	A disciple who, upon hearing one sermon from the **Buddha,** became enlightened and set out to search for the robes and begging bowl needed to ordain as a **bhikkhu.** But because of past **karma,** he was unable to

obtain these requisites and was gored to death by a cow protecting her calf.

Bhikkhu *(Pali)* A **Buddhist** monk. Literally, one who begs. Bhikkhus are not allowed to own property and are encouraged to live a life of wandering, subsisting on the gifts of lay-people. They will often teach **dharma** and officiate at ceremonies that help lay devotees gain **karmic** merit, but their primary responsibility is to work toward their own enlightenment.

Bodhi Tree *(Pali, Skt)* The tree of awakening (bodhi), under which the **Buddha** meditated during his enlightenment. A descendant of the original fig tree *(Ficus religiosa)* is still venerated in the town of Bodh Gaya in northern India, on the spot where Buddha was enlightened.

Bodhisattva *(Skt)* Literally, enlightenment being. One who is perfecting virtue with the goal of achieving **Buddhahood** through compassion and wisdom. A Bodhisattva renounces final entry into **nirvāṇa** until all other sentient beings are enlightened. The ideal in **Mahāyāna Buddhism**, as opposed to the **arahant** ideal in **Theravāda** Buddhism.

Brāhmaṇa *(Pali, Skt)*, Brahmin *(Eng)* A member of the priestly caste, the highest of the four main classes in traditional ancient Indian society and religion. The term was often used provocatively in early **Buddhist** writings to refer to any person leading a life of virtue and purity, regardless of birth.

Buddha, Buddhas
(Pali, Skt)

Literally, one who has been awakened; that is to say, enlightened. A Buddha differs from an **arahant** in that a Buddha achieves the goal without the aid of an enlightened teacher, whereas the arahant must follow the teachings of a Buddha. Because of training over countless lifetimes, a Buddha is attributed the perfection of certain powers helpful in teaching others, and, in **Mahāyāna Buddhism,** a more perfect enlightenment. From the earliest traditions, there have been stated to be many Buddhas past and future; later traditions also hold that there are currently Buddhas on other worlds or planes. In the texts, the term was frequently used as an epithet for **Gautama,** the founder of the religious movement now referred to as Buddhism.

Buddhahood *(Eng)*

The state of perfect enlightenment of a **Buddha.**

Buddha-nature *(Eng)*

In **Mahāyāna Buddhism,** the underlying essence of all beings that is both the potential for **Buddhahood** and the perfection that is present, but obscured, in the unenlightened.

Buddhism *(Eng)*

The doctrines attributed to **Gautama** and the religious practices based on those doctrines.

Buddhist *(Eng)*	A quaint person who seeks wisdom in strange ways, using no-mind to search for no-self, declaring emptiness to be Truth and extinction to be Liberation.
Dhamma *(Pali)*, Dharma *(Skt)*	Truth or ultimate law; **Buddha's** doctrines, which concern this truth; and any phenomenal manifestation whatsoever, either physical or mental. Though it is not possible to translate into an English equivalent because of the diverse and complex use of this word, common renderings include *truth, law, universal law, nature, essence, norm, doctrine, teachings, word of the Buddha, element, phenomena, thing.*
Eh Ma! *(Tib)*	An exclamation of astonishment or wonder.
Eightfold Path *(Eng)*	The eight categories of practice that lead to enlightenment:

1. Right Understanding.
2. Right Thought.
3. Right Speech.
4. Right Action.
5. Right Livelihood.
6. Right Effort.
7. Right Mindfulness.
8. Right Concentration.

Gautama *(Skt)*	The family name of the historical **Buddha.** All early accounts say he lived eighty years, though those tradi-

tions are not in agreement as to which years they were; 623–543 B.C., 566–486 B.C., and 448–368 B.C. are the most likely candidates. He was the son of Suddhodana, chieftain of the Śākya tribe, whose capital was Kapilavastu in what is now Nepal. Even after living twenty-nine years in royal luxury, married and the father of a son, Gautama was still repelled by a life that leads to old age, sickness, and death. He renounced the life of a householder and set off to find a life beyond suffering and death. At the age of thirty-five, after six years of searching, he realized perfect enlightenment, becoming a Buddha. He spent the next forty-five years traveling around the middle Ganges teaching **dharma.** His teachings are recorded in collections of sutras that vary from tradition to tradition. He died of food poisoning.

Karma *(Skt)*

Literally, action. All actions will have consequences (whether good, bad, or neutral) that are determined by the intention of those actions. If performing an action with desire for the fruit of that action, the volition itself will bind the doer to the world. Therefore, only actions that are without desire, aversion, or delusion are without karmic fruit. The doctrine of karma is a middle path between determinism and free will, since it is our previous actions that determine our current situation, but we are ultimately free in how we respond to our current situation.

Koan *(Jpn)*	In **Zen,** a paradoxical short story or phrase used as a teaching tool to suspend intellectual problem solving and dualistic thinking. A Zen master will instruct a student with a koan in order to give the student an initial enlightenment experience or to test and develop an earlier experience.
Kusa Grass *(Pali)*	*Eragrostis cynosuroides,* a tall grass with pointed leaves, sacred to both **Buddhists** and Hindus. A gift of kusa grass was given to the **Buddha** to sit on while meditating under the **Bodhi Tree.**
Mahāyāna *(Skt)*	A group of **Buddhist** sects common in central and east Asia, distinguished by the **bodhisattva** ideal and the view of **Buddha** as a universal essence. The boundaries between the Mahāyāna and other schools have not always been clear (particularly in ancient India and modern Vietnam), but a different emphasis on the role of compassion and on the emptiness of everyday reality is observed.
Māra *(Pali, Skt),* King of Death, Lord of Death, The Evil One *(Eng)*	The deification of the qualities of mind that bind us to **saṃsāra,** the cycle of life and death. He is portrayed in the scriptures as a demon creating obstacles to enlightenment for meditators. Māra is the Lord of Death, as **Buddha** is the Lord of the deathless, i.e., **nirvāṇa.**

Meghiya *(Pali)*	A disciple of the **Buddha** who was also his personal attendant at some point before **Ānanda** took the job permanently. He became enlightened after hearing a sermon from the Buddha on the conditions conducive to enlightenment.
Nāgasena *(Pali)*	(ca. second century B.C.) An enlightened monk known only from his apocryphal conversations with the Greek King Menander ("Milinda" in Pali), recorded in the Milindapañha.
Nibbāna *(Pali)*, Nirvāṇa *(Skt)*	The highest goal in **Buddhism**. A state described as peace, bliss, freedom, liberation, release, extinction, uncaused, unconditioned, void, absolute, permanent, and deathless. It is without greed, hatred, delusion, suffering, or the conceit "I am." After death, an enlightened being is said to enter final nirvāṇa, which is neither continued conditioned existence nor annihilation. In **Theravāda** Buddhism, it is seen as transcendent, wholly different from **saṃsāra**. In **Mahāyāna** Buddhism, it is seen as being identical with the true nature of saṃsāra, i.e., void.
Noble Truths *(Eng)*	The four noble truths are the heart of **Buddhist** philosophy: 1. All conditioned existence is dukkha, usually translated as unsatisfactoriness or suffering. 2. The cause of dukkha is craving.

3. The elimination of craving is the elimination of dukkha—the state known as **nirvāṇa**.
4. The **Buddha's** teachings describe the path that leads to the elimination of dukkha, known as the **eightfold path**.

Pure Land *(Eng)*

In **Mahāyāna Buddhism,** the western paradise of **Buddha Amitābha.** Followers of the Pure Land schools of Buddhism believe that anyone who earnestly invokes the name of Amitābha will be reborn in his Land of Bliss, where there is no suffering and where **nirvāṇa** will be easily attained.

Samādhi *(Pali, Skt)*

Concentration or one-pointedness of mind. Though present as the unifying function of all consciousness, there are differing levels of intensity possible, up to and including the nondual absorption attained through concentration meditation. See also **Vipassanā-bhāvanā.**

Samaṇa *(Pali)*

A wandering ascetic, whether **Buddhist** or not, whose practices are outside the mainstream **brāhmaṇa** customs.

Saṃsāra *(Pali, Skt)*

Literally, confluence. The cycle of birth, old age, affliction, and death, flowing again and again to rebirth from an unknowable beginning. The river or ocean of saṃsāra is crossed with the raft of **dharma** to the further shore of **nirvāṇa,** its opposite. Based on one's

karma, rebirth takes place on any of the planes of existence, from the lowest hell realms, through animal and human worlds, to the highest heavens as gods, and back again. In **Mahāyāna Buddhism,** saṃsāra as phenomenal existence is shown to be void and therefore paradoxically identical with nirvāṇa.

Saṃskāra *(Skt)* — Any compounded or determined thing, as opposed to unconditioned **nirvāṇa.** Often used more narrowly as mental formation.

Sangha *(Pali)* — The order of **bhikkhus** who have attained some level of enlightenment, or more widely speaking, the order of bhikkhus in general, or any community of **Buddhists,** either monastic or lay.

Sāriputta *(Pali),* Śāriputra *(Skt)* — The chief disciple of the **Buddha** and foremost in wisdom, second only to the Buddha. He was seven or eight years younger than the Buddha and died six months before the Buddha.

Sāvatthi *(Pali)* — One of the great cities of ancient India; the capital of the kingdom of Kosala. During the forty-five years after his enlightenment, **Buddha** spent twenty-five annual rainy-season retreats there.

Śākyamuni *(Skt)* — An epithet of **Gautama Buddha;** literally, "sage of the Śākya tribe."

Siddhārtha *(Skt)*	Given name of **Gautama,** but since this translates as "one who has reached the goal," it is more likely an epithet. The name was also used by Hermann Hesse in his novel *Siddhartha,* where the title character meets Gautama but chooses a different path.
Sixth Patriarch *(Eng)*	(638–713) Title of Hui-neng, a Chinese **Zen (Ch'an)** master and considered the founder of Zen **Buddhism,** the first truly Chinese form of Buddhism.
Suchness *(Eng)*	Pure being, without the superimposition or manipulation of thought constructions. It is uncaused, without form, and without self.
Tathāgata *(Pali, Skt)*	An epithet of any enlightened being and the name that **Gautama Buddha** most often used in referring to himself. The origin is obscure, but the most common interpretations are "thus gone"—referring to one who has traveled the path to enlightenment; and "one who has attained to **suchness**"—that is to say, ultimate reality.
Theravāda *(Pali)*	School of **Buddhism** common in south and southeast Asia characterized by doctrinal conservatism and the importance of monasticism. **Gautama Buddha** is seen as a human who has transcended suffering and has shown the way to become an **arahant,** like himself, through insight into the four **noble truths.**

Three Realms *(Eng)*	The **saṃsāric** realms of sensuality, fine material form, and formlessness that correspond to levels of meditative consciousness. The realm of sensuality includes rebirth in the hells, animal worlds, human worlds, and the lower heavenly worlds; all of these correspond to everyday consciousness. The realm of fine material form includes rebirth in the higher heavenly worlds, which correspond to certain high levels of concentration meditation. The realm of formless existence is accessible through the mastery of extremely high levels of meditative concentration.
Ts'ao-shan *(Chi)*	(840–901) Chinese monk and **Ch'an (Zen)** master. Student and **Dharma** successor of **Tung-shan.**
Tung-shan *(Chi)*	(807–869) Chinese monk and **Ch'an (Zen)** master. Cofounder, along with **Ts'ao-shan,** of the Ts'ao-tung school (later called Sōtō in Japan) of Ch'an **Buddhism.** Emphasized the integration of absolute and relative experience for true understanding of reality.
Vipassanā-bhāvanā *(Pali)*	The cultivation of insight. Specifically, the clear vision developed through the direct experience of the true nature of reality. It is not an intellectual process but the meditation on the impermanent, unsatisfactory, and impersonal nature of all phenomena. Insight medita-

tion and concentration meditation (**samādhi**) are the two classes of meditation in the **Buddhist** system of mental development.

Visākhā *(Pali)*

The chief female lay disciple in ministering to the **Sangha.** She is said to have given fantastic quantities of the requisites to the Sangha over many lifetimes and was the inheritor of inconceivably good karmic fruit during her lifetime. Because of her generosity and her frequent visits to the **Buddha,** she is the focus of many stories in the texts.

Wat Pah Pong *(Thai)*

A forest monastery in northeast Thailand formed in 1954 around **Ahjahn Chah,** and until his death in 1992, his main residence. The simple lifestyle, work, and strict discipline are as much a part of the practice as the periods of formal meditation.

Yogin *(Skt)*

One who practices mental training or discipline.

Zen *(Jpn)*, Ch'an *(Chi)*

A school of **Mahāyāna Buddhism** that evolved in the sixth and seventh centuries in China, influenced heavily by indigenous Taoism. It flourished in Japan starting in the twelfth century, extending to the present day, and continues to be popular in Korea and Vietnam. Zen emphasizes the direct experience of enlightenment (satori) through meditation, and the master-disciple relationship; and though scholarship and textual study are parts of Zen practice, they are, more than in any other school of Buddhism, seen as possible obstacles to enlightenment if the disciple becomes attached to the intellectual process.

BIBLIOGRAPHY

Anguttara-Nikāya, translated as *Gradual Sayings* (5 volumes). F. L. Woodward (translator). Pali Text Society, Oxford 1932–1936. (nos. *33, 35, 199, 222, 322, 362*)

Being Peace. Thich Nhat Hanh. Parallax Press, Berkeley 1987. (nos. *51, 213, 259*)

Bodhicaryāvatāra. Śantideva; Kate Crosby and Andrew Skilton (translators). Oxford University Press, Oxford 1995. (nos. *3, 41, 81, 110, 197, 275, 300*)

Bodhicaryāvatāra (same as *Bodhisattvacharyavatara*), translated as *Guide to the Bodhisattva's Way of Life.* Shantideva; Stephen Batchelor (translator). Library of Tibetan Works & Archives, Dharamshala 1979. (nos. *45, 58, 170, 203, 207, 239, 359*)

Bodhicaryāvatāra (same as *Bodhisattvacharyavatara*), translated with oral commentary as *Meaningful to Behold.* Shantideva; commentary by Geshe Kelsang Gyatso; Tenzin Norbu (translator). Wisdom Publications, Ulverston 1980. (nos. *14, 17, 61, 165*)

Bodhicaryāvatāra, translated as *Way of the Bodhisattva.* Shāntideva; the Padmakara Translation Group (translators). Shambhala Publications, Boston 1997. (nos. *23, 52, 66, 114, 140, 184*)

Bodhinyāna: A Collection of Dhamma Talks. Ajahn Chah; The Sangha, Bung Wai Forest Monastery (translators). The Sangha, Bung Wai

Forest Monastery, Ubon Rajathani Province (Thailand) 1982. (nos. *1, 78, 88*)

Buddhist Wisdom Books: Containing the Diamond Sutra and the Heart Sutra. Edward Conze (translator and commentator). George Allen & Unwin, Ltd., London 1958; reprinted by Harper & Row, New York 1972. (no. *62*)

Cutting Through Spiritual Materialism. Chögyam Trungpa. Shambhala Publications, Boston 1973. (nos. *151, 323, 332*)

Dhammapada, 3rd edition. Nārada Thera (translator). Buddhist Missionary Society, Kuala Lumpur 1978. (nos. *150, 178, 219, 237, 258, 313, 321*)

Dhammapada: The Buddha's Path of Wisdom, 2nd edition, Acharya Buddharakkhita (translator). Buddhist Publication Society, Kandy 1996. (nos. *16, 27, 121, 147, 231, 266*)

Dhammapada Commentary, translated as *Buddhist Legends.* Eugene Watson Burlingame (translator). Harvard University Press, Cambridge 1921; reprinted by Pali Text Society, London 1990. (nos. *10, 13, 67, 79, 134, 154, 159, 166, 171, 194, 198, 204, 215, 255, 270*)

Dhammapada: The Path of Truth. Balangoda Ananda Maitreya (translator); revised by Rose Kramer. Lotsawa, Novato (California) 1988. (nos. *34, 46, 91, 127, 188, 262, 325*)

Dhammapada: The Sayings of the Buddha. Thomas Byrom (translator). Alfred A. Knopf, New York 1976. (nos. *2, 53, 225, 276, 282, 305, 336*)

Dhammapada: Wisdom of the Buddha. Harischandra Kaviratna (translator). Theosophical University Press, Pasadena 1980. (nos. *82, 183, 248, 329, 357*)

Diamond Sutra and The Sutra of Hui Neng. A. F. Price and Wong Mou-Lam (translators). Shambhala Publications, Boulder (Colorado) 1969. (nos. *9, 31, 36, 54, 101, 115, 145, 155, 185, 247, 310, 349, 358*)

Dīgha Nikāya, translated as *Thus Have I Heard.* Maurice Walshe (translator). Wisdom Publications, London 1987. (nos. *72, 100, 107, 119, 192, 284*)

Drinking the Mountain Stream: Songs of Tibet's Beloved Saint, Milarepa, revised edition. Lama Kunga Rinpoche and Brian Cutillo (translators). Wisdom Publications, Boston 1995. (nos. *30, 40, 87, 181, 233, 240, 330, 343, 354*)

Essence of Mahayana Lojong Practice: An Oral Commentary to Geshe Langri Tangpa's Mind Training *in Eight Verses.* Sermey Geshe Lobsang Tharchin. Mahayana Sutra and Tantra Press, Howell (New Jersey) 1998. (nos. *103, 211*)

First Buddhist Women: Translations and Commentaries on the Therigatha. Susan Murcott. Parallax Press, Berkeley 1991. (nos. *55, 156*)

Five Houses of Zen. Thomas Cleary (translator). Shambhala Publications, Boston 1997. (nos. *75, 148, 187, 201, 221, 254, 316*)

Flowers Fall: A Commentary on Dōgen's Genjōkōan. Hakuun Yasutani; Paul Jaffe (translator). Shambhala Publications, Boston 1996. (nos. *80, 164, 297*)

Fo-sho-hing-tsan-king, A Life of the Buddha, a translation/paraphrase of Aśvaghosha's Sanskrit *Buddhacarita* into Chinese. Samuel Beal (translator from Chinese to English). Oxford University Press, Oxford 1883; reprinted by Motilal Banarsidass, Delhi 1984. (nos. *6, 20, 26, 32, 42, 60, 70, 77, 89, 92, 97, 104, 109, 124, 131, 133, 136, 142, 149, 163, 168, 182, 190, 196, 202, 220, 224, 245, 251, 256, 283, 293, 312, 341*)

Guide to Walking Meditation. Thich Nhat Hanh; Jenny Hoang and Nguyen Anh Huong (translators). Fellowship Publications, Nyack (New York) 1985. (no. *25*)

Heart Released. Phra Ajaan Mun Bhūridatta Thera; (translator unknown). Thailand (publisher, city, and date unknown). (nos. *269, 315*)

Hundred Thousand Songs of Milarepa (2 volumes). Garma C. C. Chang (translator). University Books, New Hyde Park (New York) 1962. (nos. *4, 21, 71, 129, 135, 146, 167, 229 246, 250, 327, 337, 364*)

Hundred Thousand Songs: Selections from Milarepa, Poet-Saint of Tibet. Antoinette K. Gordon (translator). Charles E. Tuttle Company, Rutland (Vermont) and Tokyo 1961. (nos. *177, 208, 218, 268, 309, 360*)

Itivuttaka: As It Was Said, translated in *Minor Anthologies of the Pali Canon,* part II. F. L. Woodward (translator). Pali Text Society, London 1935; reprinted 1987. (nos. *24, 244, 257, 286*)

Itivuttaka: The Buddha's Sayings. John D. Ireland (translator). Buddhist

Publication Society, Kandy 1991. (nos. *76, 132, 157, 230, 238, 335*)

Living Dhamma. Ajahn Chah; (translator unknown). Saṅgha, Bung Wai Forest Monastery, Ubon Rajathani (Thailand) 1992. (nos. *111, 118, 261, 298*)

Majjhima-Nikāya, translated as *Middle Length Discourses of the Buddha.* Bhikkhu Ñāṇamoli, and Bhikkhu Bodhi (translators). Wisdom Publications, Boston 1995. (nos. *18, 186, 217, 287, 345*)

Milindapañha, translated as *Milinda's Questions* (2 volumes). I. B. Horner (translator). Pali Text Society, 1963 (vol. I) and 1964 (vol. 2); reprinted Pali Text Society, Oxford 1996. (no. *291*)

Milindapañha, translated as *The Questions of King Milinda* (2 volumes). T. W. Rhys Davids (translator). In *The Sacred Books of the East,* vols. 35 and 36. F. Max Müller (editor). Clarendon Press, Oxford 1890 (vol. 35) and 1894 (vol. 36); reprinted by Dover Publications, New York 1963. (nos. *8, 43, 49, 59, 64, 84, 98, 102, 116, 173, 206, 227, 234, 241, 249, 272, 333, 342, 350*)

Mind Like Fire Unbound. Thanissaro Bhikkhu. Dhamma Dana Publications, Barre (Massachusetts) 1993. (nos. *274, 290, 347*)

Mind of Clover: Essays in Zen Buddhist Ethics. Robert Aitken. North Point Press, San Francisco 1984. (nos. *74, 141, 331, 363*)

Mindfulness in Plain English. Venerable Henepola Gunaratana. Wisdom Publications, Somerville (Massachusetts) 1992. (nos. *162, 303*)

Miracle of Mindfulness! Thich Nhat Hanh; Mobi Warren (translator). Beacon Press, Boston 1975. (nos. *125, 193, 253*)

Moon in a Dewdrop: Writings of Zen Master Dōgen. Kazuaki Tanahashi, (editor). North Point Press, New York 1985. (nos. *22, 289, 361*)

Mūlamadhyamaka-kārikā, translated as *Fundamental Wisdom of the Middle Way.* Nāgārjuna; Jay L. Garfield (translator). Oxford University Press, New York 1995. (nos. *19, 48, 56, 95, 108, 153, 191, 200, 205, 216, 348, 353*)

Power of Mindfulness. Nyanaponika Thera. Buddhist Publication Society, Kandy 1968; revised 1986. (nos. *160, 175, 273*)

Prasannapadā, translated as *Lucid Exposition of the Middle Way.* Candrakīrti; Mervyn Sprung (translator). Routledge & Kegan Paul, London and Henley 1979. (nos. *69, 307*)

Rājaparikathāratnāvalī, translated as *Buddhist Advice for Living & Liberation: Nāgārjuna's Precious Garland.* Jeffrey Hopkins (translator). Snow Lion Publications, Ithaca (New York) 1998. (nos. *11, 63, 174, 242, 281, 296, 319, 328, 334, 344*)

Rational Zen: The Mind of Dōgen Zenji. Thomas Cleary (translator). Shambhala Publications, Boston 1992; reprinted 1995. (nos. *15, 99, 232, 294, 306, 352*)

Saṃyutta Nikāya, translated as *An Anthology from the Saṃyutta Nikāya.* John D. Ireland (translator, part I); Bhikku Ñānananda (translator, part II); M. O' C. Walshe (translator, part III). Buddhist Publication Society, Kandy 1981–1985. (nos. *37, 126, 228, 236*)

Saṃyutta Nikāya, translated as *The Book of the Kindred Sayings* (5 volumes). Mrs. Rhys Davids and F. L. Woodward (translators). Pali Text Society, Oxford 1917–1930. (no. *44*)

Saṃyutta Nikāya, translated as *Three Cardinal Discourses of the Buddha.* Ñāṇamoli Thera (translator). Buddhist Publication Society, Kandy 1981. (no. *299*)

Seeing the Way. Ajahn Chah, et al.; (editor and translator unknown). Amaravati Publications, Hemel Hempstead (Hertfordshire, England) 1989. (nos. *120, 279, 356*)

Seven Contemplations of Insight. Venerable Mātara Śri Ñāṇārāma Mahāthera. Buddhist Publication Society, Kandy 1997. (no. *158*)

Siddhartha. Hermann Hesse; Hilda Rosner (translator). New Directions, New York 1951; reprinted Bantam, New York 1971. (no. *143*)

Still Forest Pool: The Insight Meditation of Achaan Chah. Jack Kornfield and Paul Breiter (compilers and editors). Quest (Theosophical Publishing House), Wheaton (Illinois) 1985. (nos. *50, 105, 139, 152, 172, 209, 340*)

Sutta Nipāta. H. Saddhātissa (translator). Curzon Press, London 1985. (nos. *12, 47, 138, 189, 210, 285, 314, 338*)

Sutta Nipāta, translated as *The Discourse Collection: Selected Texts from the Sutta Nipāta.* John D. Ireland (translator). Buddhist Publication Society, Kandy 1965; reprinted 1983. (nos. *57, 65, 86, 179, 195, 295*)

Sutta Nipāta, translated as *The Rhinoceros Horn and Other Early Buddhist Poems.* K. R. Norman (translator); with alternative translations by I. B. Horner and Walpola Rahula. Pali Text Society, London 1985. (nos. *29, 112, 117, 123, 265*)

Sutta Nipāta, translated as *The Worn-out Skin: Contemplations on the Uraga Sutta of the Sutta Nipāta*. Nyanaponika Thera (translator). Buddhist Publication Society, Kandy 1977; reprinted in *The Vision of Dhamma*. Samuel Weiser, York Beach (Maine) 1987. (nos. *176, 243*)

Taste of Freedom: Selected Dhamma Talks. Ajahn Chah; (translator unknown). Buddhist Publication Society, Kandy 1988. (nos. *38, 128, 144, 212, 304*)

Udāna, translated as *80 Inspiring Words of the Buddha*. Bhadragaka (translator), Bangkok 1954 (publisher unknown). (nos. *83, 252, 326*)

Udāna: Inspired Utterances of the Buddha. John D. Ireland (translator). Buddhist Publication Society, Kandy 1990. (nos. *96, 106, 180, 264, 318, 320*)

Udāna or The Solemn Utterances of the Buddha. D. M. Strong (translator). Luzac & Co., London 1902. (nos. *73, 301, 324*)

Udāna: Verses of Uplift, translated in *Minor Anthologies of the Pali Canon*, part II. F. L. Woodward (translator). Pali Text Society, London 1935; reprinted 1987. (nos. *85, 308*)

Union of Mahamudra and Dzogchen. Chökyi Nyima Rinpoche; Erik Pema Kunsang (translator). Rangjung Yeshe Publications, Hong Kong 1994. (nos. *169, 288, 355*)

Venerable Father: A Life with Ahjahn Chah. Paul Breiter. Funny Publishing Ltd., Bangkok 1993. (nos. *90, 223, 267, 365*)

Visuddhimagga, translated as *Path of Purification,* 3rd edition. Bhadantācariya Buddhaghosa; Bhikkhu Ñāṇamoli (translator). Buddhist Publication Society, Kandy 1975. (nos. *130, 161, 263*)

Visuddhimagga, translated as *Path of Purity.* Buddhaghosa; Pe Maung Tin (translator). Pali Text Society, London. Parts I, II, III first published 1923, 1929, 1931 (respectively); all reprinted 1975. (no. *271*)

Wisdom of No Escape: and the Path of Loving-Kindness. Pema Chödrön. Shambhala Publications, Boston 1991. (nos. *93, 235, 339*)

Zen Master Hakuin: Selected Writings. Philip B. Yampolsky (translator). Columbia University Press, New York 1971. (nos. *39, 137, 280, 311, 351*)

Zen Mind, Beginner's Mind. Shunryu Suzuki. Weatherhill, New York 1970; reprinted 1983. (nos. *5, 28, 113, 226, 277, 302, 317*)

Zen Teaching of Huang Po. John Blofeld (translator). Grove Weidenfeld, New York 1958. (nos. *7, 68, 94, 122, 214, 260, 278, 292, 346*)